SUSPECT

JOHN LOCKE
AND THE
RYE HOUSE PLOT

The Rye House

CHRISTOPHER LOCKE

CenterLine Publishing
& Consulting LLC

2021
CenterLine Publishing & Consulting LLC
ISBN: 9798471436367

To "Good Pennyworth" . . .

I hope to visit someday.

CONTENTS

INTRODUCTION

John Locke was a prominent and influential 17th-18th century English philosopher, Oxford academic, and medical researcher. Locke is widely regarded as one of the most instrumental of the 'Enlightenment' thinkers, and is commonly known around the world as the "Father of Liberalism". Considered one of the first of the British pragmatists, Locke is considered important to the legitimacy of the authority of the state over the individual. His work greatly affected the development of political values as well as "epistemology", a branch of philosophy concerned with the nature, origin, and scope of knowledge, including knowledge validation and the rationality of belief.

John Locke's writings influenced numerous Scottish Enlightenment thinkers and American Revolutionaries - most specifically, Thomas Jefferson. Locke's contributions to classical republicanism and liberal theory are greatly reflected in the Declaration of Independence as adopted by the Second Continental Congress in Philadelphia on July 4, 1776. Internationally, and in modern times, Locke's legal-political principles continue to have an acute influence on the theory and practice of "limited representative government" and the protection of basic freedoms and rights under the rule of law.

It was the "Whig" movement, an advancement in constitutional monarchism and opposition to absolute monarchy, that exerted great influence on Locke's political ideas. The Whigs played a significant role in the "Glorious Revolution" of 1688, the last successful invasion of England and an internal coup that resulted in the overthrow of King James II and VII of England, Scotland and Ireland. Most certainly, the Whigs were the standing enemies of the prevalent kings and rulers who were Roman Catholic or, at least, were tolerant of Catholics.

On a religious level, Locke was influenced by Baptist theologians. He believed that enforcing a single 'true religion', such as Catholic convictions, would not result in the desired effect of 'true belief' since belief cannot be compelled by violence.

Certainly, Locke's political convictions and philosophy on freedom were based on his own religious beliefs and Bible interpretations. According to Locke, one of the aftermaths of the principle of 'equality' was that all human beings were created equally free and, therefore, governments, including the English monarchy, needed the consent of those being acceptingly governed.

In 1683, the King of Scotland, England, and Ireland was Charles II. His brother and heir presumptive was James, Duke of York. King Charles's English parliament enacted laws known as the "Clarendon Code", a group of penal rules designed to shore up the position of the re-established Church of England. These codes angered Whig leaders, including Locke, both politically and religiously since Charles II and brother James were not only sympathetic to Roman Catholics, but would subsequently commit themselves to Catholicism. This resentment led to the "Rye House Plot", a plan to assassinate both Charles II and James, and mount a rebellion against their dynasty's monarchy.

Helping to lead the Plot was James Scott, 1st Duke of Monmouth, and eldest illegitimate son of Charles II. Scott, Along with a number of conspirators, Scott planned the assignation to take place from the grounds of the 'Rye House', a fortified manor house located in southeast England. The plan was to ambush the King and Duke as they passed by on their way back to London from regional horse races. As fate would have it, the races were cancelled, and the King and the Duke returned to London early. As a result, the planned assassination never took place.

Nonetheless, the Plot was quickly uncovered, causing the arrests and subsequent executions of the involved Whig leaders. Other accused conspirators managed to escape to other countries. Among them were John Locke and James Scott who fled to the Netherlands. In Locke's case, there was enough evidence to support his involvement in the Plot, compelling him to literally flee for his life from England. His close association with some of the conspirators, and his willingness to arrange accommodations for them during the timeframe of the Plot certainly implicated him beyond a reasonable doubt.

Prior to the events, Locke's political relationship with James Scott allowed for the eventual immigration of one of Locke's direct relatives, Phillip, to the American Colonies, per Scott's regal authorization.

However, Phillip's blood line relationship with John Locke and the consent from Scott to immigrate created enough fear to compel Phillip to abscond to Ireland for four years before his successful travels to America.

The outcome of the failure of the Rye House Plot resulted in the implications, arrests, trials, imprisonments and, in many cases, executions, of more than 40 people. Fortunately, neither John Locke nor Phillip Lock(e) sustained any retribution from the monarchy, either physically or politically. Regardless, the suspicions of their involvement, especially of the elder John, remain to this day.

Incidentally, Phillip's historic and documented last name, at least in America, is spelled L-O-C-K, despite the evidence of his relation the Locke family. The potential reason for the missing 'E' is explained in Chapter 9 under the heading, "Phillip Lock(e); a Life in America". Given this, we will refer to Phillip during his time in England with the L-O-C-K-E spelling, then switch to the documented L-O-C-K following his arrival in America.

In great historic detail and compelling evidence, this book covers the profile, account, and motivations of each of the main characters involved in the attempt to assassinate the Charles II, the King of England, and his brother, James, heir to the throne. With special focus on world renowned English philosopher, John Locke, the book provides comprehensive insight into the mind of Locke, as well as the political and religious philosophies that tied him to the Rye House Plot, even as an ingenuous conspirator. While previous scholars supposed there was little evidence to suggest Locke was directly involved in the scheme, the book does a thorough job in connecting Locke with those who planned the King's assignation, and those who were ready to carry out the mission.

The book then follows Locke and his political colleague, James Scott, as they flee to the Netherlands to avoid arrest, trial, and probable death. The book also follows Locke's relative, Phillip, who became caught up in an adverse consequence of partisan networking, requiring his own escape from England, and his eventual journey to America.

The account of the Rye House Plot would make for an intriguing and captivating fiction novel, except the facts of the storyline are categorically true and thoroughly documented. The narrative is a mix of 17th century espionage, greed, providence, and radical ideology, whose insight is uniquely presented with information not previously known by earlier historians. The basis of this exclusive insight is due to the fact that Phillip Lock(e) was my 7th-Great Grandfather. His biography and affiliation with John Locke and James Scott was handed down from my ancestors who conducted the initial research well before the Internet. I then expounded on that research through extensive documentation and investigations, as well as DNA testing and family tree verifications. The result is this fascinating and never-before known story of the politically-charged John Locke and his involvement in the attempted assignation of a British king. It is my sincere hope that you, the reader, will find this historic chronicle as interesting, surprising, and provocative as I have.

CHRISTOPHER LOCKE

SUSPECT

JOHN LOCKE
AND THE
RYE HOUSE PLOT

PART ONE: THE PLAYERS

CHAPTER 1:
JOHN LOCKE

Introduction

John Locke was an English philosopher and physician who is often considered the "Father of Liberalism" and one of the most significant Enlightenment theorists. Locke is similarly essential to social contract theory as one of the first British empiricists, following in the footsteps of Sir Francis Bacon. His work had a significant impact on epistemology and political philosophy. Voltaire and Jean-Jacques Rousseau, as well as numerous Scottish Enlightenment philosophers and American Revolutionaries, were affected by his writings. The United States Declaration of Independence acknowledges his contributions to classical republicanism and liberal ideology. Locke's political-legal principles have had a lasting impact on the theory and practice of limited representative government and the safeguarding of fundamental rights and freedoms under the rule of law around the world.

Locke's theory of mind is frequently credited with establishing contemporary concepts of identity and the self, with other thinkers such as Jean-Jacques Rousseau, David Hume, and Immanuel Kant citing it as a major influence. Locke was the first to define the self in terms of awareness continuity. He proposed that the mind was a blank slate, or tabula rasa, at birth. In contrast to Cartesian philosophy, he claimed that we are born without innate ideas and that knowledge is decided solely by experience gained from sense perception, a view now known as empiricism. In his findings, he demonstrates the scientific idea that something must be able to be tested repeatedly and that nothing is immune to being disproved. Locke once stated, *"Whatever I write, as soon as I discover it not to be true, my hand shall be the forwardest to throw it into the fire".*

Birth, Beginnings & Education

John Locke was born in a small, thatched cottage near a church in Wrington, Somerset, about 12 miles from Bristol, on August 29,

1632. Because both of his parents were Puritans, he was baptized on the same day. Locke's father, also named John, was an attorney who worked as a clerk for the Justices of the Peace in Chew Magna and as a cavalry commander for Parliamentarian forces during the English Civil War's early stages. Agnes Keene was his mother. Locke's family relocated to the market town of Pensford, some seven miles south of Bristol, shortly after his birth, where he grew up in a rural Tudor mansion in Belluton.

Under the support of Alexander Popham, a member of Parliament and John's former commander, Locke was sent to the prestigious Westminster School in London in 1647. He was admitted to Christ Church, Oxford, in the autumn of 1652, at the age of 20, after finishing his studies there. John Owen, vice-chancellor of the university, was the dean of the college at the time. Locke was a capable student, but the undergraduate curriculum of the period frustrated him. Modern philosophers' works, such as René Descartes', he found more engaging than the classical material given at university. Locke was introduced to medicine and the experimental philosophy being studied at other universities and in the Royal Society, where he eventually became a member, through his friend Richard Lower, whom he knew from the Westminster School.

In February 1656, Locke received his bachelor's degree, and in June 1658, he received his master's degree. In February 1675, he received a Bachelor of Medicine after studying the subject thoroughly during his stay at Oxford and working with notable scientists and intellectuals such as Robert Boyle, Thomas Willis, and Robert Hooke, in addition to Lower.

Post-Graduation

In 1666, John met Anthony Ashley Cooper, the Lord of Shaftsbury, aka "Lord Ashley", as he will be referred to for the remainder of the book. Ashley was a leading English politician during the reign of King Charles II. Ashley was seeking treatment for a liver illness and had travelled to Oxford. He was pleased with Locke's result in treating him, and convinced him to join his entourage, and serving as a patron of Locke's.

Locke was seeking for work and moved into Ashley's home at Exeter House in London in 1667 to work as his personal physician.

Locke resumed his medical studies in London under the supervision of Thomas Sydenham. Locke's natural philosophical thought was profoundly influenced by Sydenham, as evidenced in "An Essay Concerning Human Understanding".

When Ashley's liver ailment grew life-threatening, Locke's medical knowledge was put to the test. Locke undoubtedly had a key role in encouraging Ashley to have surgery to remove the cyst (which was life-threatening at the time). Ashley made it through and prospered, praising Locke for saving his life.

Through Ashley, Locke had positions as Secretary of the Board of Trade and Plantations and Secretary to the Lords Proprietors of Carolina during this time, which influenced his views on international trade and economics.

Besides being a mentor, Ashley had a significant influence on Locke's political ideals as a pioneer of the Whig movement. In the parliaments of England, Scotland, Great Britain, Ireland, and the United Kingdom, the Whigs were a political faction and, then, a political party. Between the 1680s until the 1850s, the Tories and the Whigs battled for control. In the 1850s, the Whigs amalgamated with the nascent Liberal Party, however some Whig aristocrats withdrew in 1885 to create the Liberal Unionist Party, which merged with the Liberals' competitor, the modern-day Conservative Party, in 1912.

The Whigs' origin lay in constitutional monarchism and opposition to absolute monarchy, supporting a parliamentary system. The Whigs played a central role in the "Glorious Revolution of 1688" (to be described later) and were the standing enemies of the Stuart kings and pretenders, who were Roman Catholic.

When Ashley became Lord Chancellor in 1672, Locke became interested in politics. In 1673, Ashley was also made 1st Earl of Shaftesbury. Locke spent considerable time traveling across France as a tutor and medical attendant to Caleb Banks after Ashley's demise in 1675. When Ashley's political prospects improved briefly in 1679, Locke returned to England. When Ashley, split with King Charles and became leader of the opposing Whigs, Locke supported, if not wrote, a pamphlet critical of the King's policies which was condemned and to be burned by the hangman. This is the first documented evidence of Locke's contempt for the British monarchy as it was control at that time, especially one of such graphic endorsement.

Locke wrote the bulk of the "Two Treatises of Government" during this period, most likely at Ashley's request. While it was traditionally assumed that Locke authored the Treatises to defend the Glorious Revolution of 1688, current research has revealed that the work was written far earlier. Individual agreement as the basis of political legitimacy is increasingly seen as a broader argument against absolute monarchy. Despite his association with the powerful Whigs, Locke's ideas regarding natural rights and government are nevertheless regarded innovative for the time period.

Formation of Ideas

In order to understand the motivation of John Locke's involvement in the Rye House Plot, we must examine his beginnings and basis of thought, ideas, and theories that continued well past the events of 1683. Locke was much more than an observer of what was taking place around him. Despite his relaxed and generally mild demeanor, he could be easily consumed with rage when occurrences affected (or could affect) his life and general wellbeing, as well as that of others. Taking action and proactive measures in the company of those who shared his views made Locke a leader, but an obscure one. He was not the first draw a sword, but he was the one to justify the actions of others when they met with his own beliefs. And while some of the following topics are not directly related to politics or religion which led to the Rye House Plot, they still offer an insight into Locke's thought process and strong beliefs of government versus self.

Locke's Two Treatises were infrequently quoted throughout the late 17th and early 18th centuries. Even as a contribution to the fierce debate of the 1690s, it had little influence and was mostly disregarded until 1703, though it was supposed to have created "a tremendous commotion" in Oxford in 1695. No one, including most Whigs, was ready for the idea of a notional or abstract contract of the kind adumbrated by Locke in the early phases of the Glorious Revolution, up until 1692, and even less after that, unless it was to heap scorn on them. Indeed, Algernon Sidney's "Discourses Concerning Government" had a far greater impact than Locke's "Two Treatises."

Due to their revolutionary content, The Two Treatises were only reprinted once in the 50 years following Queen Anne's death in

1714. The Second Treatise of Government, on the other hand, received a new audience as American resistance to British taxation grew. It was extensively mentioned in both American and British debates. The first printing in America took place in Boston in 1773.

Locke had a significant impact on political thought, particularly contemporary liberalism. By tempering Hobbesian absolutism and explicitly dividing the spheres of Church and State, Locke established liberalism. Voltaire dubbed him "le sage Locke" because of his profound influence. Alexander Hamilton, James Madison, Thomas Jefferson, and other Founding Fathers of the United States were affected by his theories about liberty and the social contract. In fact, one sentence from the Second Treatise, the allusion to a *"long train of abuses"*, is quoted directly in the Declaration of Independence. Locke had such an impact on Thomas Jefferson that he wrote the following: *"Bacon, Locke and Newton . . . I consider them as the three greatest men that have ever lived, without any exception, and as having laid the foundation of those superstructures which have been raised in the Physical and Moral sciences."*

In the field of epistemology, though, Locke's influence may have been much greater. Leading intellectual historians claim that Locke's "An Essay Concerning Human Understanding" represents the beginning of the current Western understanding of the self since it redefined subjectivity.

The subject matter of modern psychology has been greatly affected by Locke's theory of association. Other philosophers were inspired by Locke's observation of two sorts of ideas, basic and complex, and their interplay through associationism to update and develop this theory and use it to explain how humans gain knowledge in the physical world at the time.

Ideas on Religious Tolerance

When writing his "Letters Concerning Toleration" between 1689 and 1692, and in the aftermath of the European wars of religion, Locke formulated a classic reasoning for religious tolerance, in which three arguments are central:

1. Earthly judges, the state in particular, and humans in general, are unable to reliably evaluate conflicting religious viewpoints' truth claims.

2. Even if they could, establishing a single "true religion" would be ineffective since belief cannot be forced through violence.
3. More social chaos would result from enforcing religious uniformity than from tolerating variance.

Baptist theologians who issued tracts advocating religious freedom of conscience in the early 17th century affected Locke's views on religious tolerance. Roger Williams, a Baptist theologian, created the colony of Rhode Island in 1636 by combining a democratic government with unrestricted religious liberty. His tract, "The Bloudy Tenent of Persecution for Cause of Conscience," was a passionate argument for religious freedom and utter separation of church and state that was widely read in the native country. Martin Luther refused to retract his beliefs before the Holy Roman Empire's Diet of Worms in 1521 until the Bible proved him wrong.

Religion was second only to politics when it came to fueling Locke's passion against the British monarch under Charles II. It seems somewhat hypocritical, though, for Locke to support religious tolerance while the Whigs condemned Catholics and King's Charle's seeming forbearance for Catholics.

Ideas of Slavery & Child Labor

Despite his genius, Locke's ideas weren't perfect, and some were far from today's social consciousness and morality. But to be fair, judging someone's thoughts and actions who lived over 300 years ago against today's acceptance is heartless and cowardice.

Slavery was a broad and complex issue for Locke. Despite his writings against slavery in general, Locke was a shareholder and beneficiary of the slave-trading Royal Africa Company. Furthermore, while serving as secretary to Lord Ashley, Locke helped draft the Fundamental Constitutions of Carolina, which established a quasi-feudal aristocracy and gave Carolinian planters absolute power over their enslaved chattel property. The constitutions stated that "every freeman of Carolina shall have absolute power and authority over his negro slaves." As a secretary to the Council of Trade and Plantations and a member of the Board of Trade, Locke was "one of just half a dozen persons who designed and managed both the colonies and their iniquitous systems of enslavement," according to philosopher Martin Cohen.

According to American historian James Farr, Locke never voiced any feelings about his opposing views on slavery, which he attributed to his personal involvement in the slave trade. Locke's views on slavery have been characterized as hypocritical, and he is credited with laying the groundwork for the Founding Fathers to hold similar contradictory views on freedom and slavery. In addition, Locke prepared implementing instructions for the Carolina colonists to guarantee that settlement and development complied with the Fundamental Constitutions. The Grand Model for the Province of Carolina is the name given to all of these papers taken together.

Historian Holly Brewer, on the other hand, claims that Locke's role in the Carolina Constitution was inflated, and that he was only paid to modify and copy a document that had already been completed in part before Locke got involved. She likens Locke's job to that of a lawyer drafting a will. She also mentions that Locke was paid in Royal African Company stock rather than cash for his employment as a secretary for a government subcommittee, and that he sold the shares after only a few years. Brewer also claims that while serving as the president of a Board of Trade established by William of Orange following the Glorious Revolution, Locke actively fought to undermine slavery in Virginia. To undermine a primary rationale for slavery—that enslaved Africans were heathens with no rights—he explicitly challenged imperial policy awarding land to slave owners and advocated the baptism and Christian education of the children of enslaved Africans.

Like most people living in the 15th and 16th century, Locke supported child labor. In his writing, "Essay on the Poor Law," he turns to the education of the poor by stating, *"The children of laboring people are an ordinary burden to the parish, and are usually maintained in idleness, so that their labor also is generally lost to the public till they are 12 or 14 years old."* Locke therefore recommended that "working schools" be set up in each English parish for poor children *"so that they will be from three years old trained to work."* He goes on to explain the economics of these schools, suggesting that they will not only be profitable for the parish, but that they will also teach the youngsters a healthy work ethic. Here again, Locke shows his flaws as a citizen of historical Great Britain.

Theories of Property & Value

Locke employs the term "property" in both broad and restricted senses. It encompasses a vast spectrum of human desires and interests. It specifically refers to tangible goods. He contends that property is a natural right arising from work. Locke argues in Chapter V of his Second Treatise that individual ownership of things and property is justified by the labor invested in their creation . . . *"at least where there is enough, and as good, left in common for others - or use property to produce goods beneficial to human society"*.

In his "Second Treatise", Locke articulated his conviction that nature contributes little worth to society on its own, meaning that the labor put in the creation of products gives them their value. Locke established a labor theory of property based on this premise, known as a labor theory of value, in which property ownership is created by the application of labor. Furthermore, he felt that property came before government and that the government could not *"dispose of the subjects' estates arbitrarily."* In his own social theory, Karl Marx criticized Locke's idea of property. This is not surprising, considering Marxism panted the seed of tyranny in which Communist regimes produced the ultimate ideological carnage in human history, ending with the deaths of a hundred million people in the last century.

Unused property is wasteful and against nature, according to Locke, but with the emergence of "durable" products, persons might trade their extra perishable things for those that would survive longer and therefore not violate the natural law. The advent of money, in his opinion, represented the end of this process, allowing for the endless accumulation of property without incurring waste due to deterioration. He also considered gold and silver to be money since they can be "hoarded up without causing harm to anyone," as they do not deteriorate or decay in the possession of the holder. The introduction of money, in his opinion, removes the constraints to accumulation.

Locke emphasizes that inequality has arisen as a result of an unspoken agreement on the use of money, rather than the social contract that established civil society or the law of land that regulates property. Unlimited accumulation poses a dilemma for Locke, but he does not consider it his responsibility. He just suggests that government should have a role in resolving the tension between unrestricted property accumulation and a more nearly equal distribution of wealth. That being said, he did not specify which principles government should use to do so. However, his thoughts do not all come together in a coherent whole. The labor theory of value, for example, appears alongside the demand-and-supply theory of value articulated in a letter titled "Some Considerations on the Consequences of the Lowering of Interest and the Raising of the Value of Money" in his "Two Treatises of Government". Furthermore, while Locke grounds property in labor, he ultimately supports the unrestricted growth of wealth.

Ideas on Political Theory

The social compact was the foundation of Locke's political theory. The idea behind this is an implicit agreement between the members of a society to "cooperate" for certain social benefits; for example, by giving up some individual freedoms for a guarantee of state protection.

Unlike Thomas Hobbes, Locke felt that reason and tolerance are inherent in human nature. Locke, like Hobbes, believed that human nature permitted selfishness, and the introduction of cash exemplifies this. Everyone was equal and independent in a natural condition, and everyone had an inherent right to defend his "life, health, liberty, or belongings." Although alternative sources have been offered, most academics attribute the phrase "Life, Liberty, and the Pursuit of Happiness" in the American Declaration of Independence to Locke's theory of rights.

Locke, like Hobbes, believed that the mere right to defend in the state of nature was insufficient, therefore people formed a civil society to resolve conflicts in a civil manner with the assistance of the government in a state of society. Locke, on the other hand, never mentions Hobbes by name and may have been replying to other writers of the time. Locke also believed in the separation of powers in government and that "revolution" is not only a right but also a necessity in certain circumstances. Certainly, in using the term "revolution", Locke must have been accepted the idea of an upheaval in which the monarchy would be replaced, forcefully or not, or at least the form of government would be altered. These concepts would have a significant impact on the United States' Declaration of Independence and Constitution.

Views on Price Theory

Locke's general theory of value and price is a supply-and-demand theory outlined in a letter to a member of parliament titled "Some Considerations on the Consequences of the Lowering of Interest and the Raising of the Value of Money" written in 1691. He defines supply as amount and demand as rent in it: *"The price of any commodity rises or falls by the proportion of the number of buyers and sellers"*, and, *"that which regulates the price of goods is nothing else but their quantity in proportion to their rent"*.

A specific case of this general theory is the quantity theory of money. His concept is founded on "Money "answers all questions," or *"money is always plenty, or more than sufficient,"* and *"varies very little."* In the case of money, Locke finds that demand is solely governed by its quantity, regardless of whether the demand for money is boundless or constant. He also looks into the factors that influence demand and supply. He discusses the worth of products in terms of scarcity and ability to be exchanged and consumed in terms of supply. He defines demand for products as the ability to generate a stream of money.

Land, for example, has value because *"it brings in a definite yearly income through its steady production of saleable goods,"* according to Locke's early theory of capitalization. He sees money demand as being similar to that of products or land: it all depends on whether money is desired as a means of trade. As a medium of exchange, he claims that *"money is capable of procuring us the necessaries or conveniences of life by exchange,"* and for loanable funds, he claims that *"money is capable of procuring us the necessaries or conveniences of life by exchange. It becomes of the same nature as land when it generates a certain annual income, or interest."*

Monetary Theories

Money has two purposes according to Locke; as a counter to measure value and as a commitment to lay claim to assets. He believes that silver and gold, rather than paper money, should be used in international transactions. He claims that silver and gold are treated equally by all of humanity and hence may be used as a commitment by anybody, whereas the worth of paper money is only legitimate under the government that provides it.

Locke says that a country should strive for a good trade balance in order to avoid falling behind other countries and losing trade. Because the world's money supply rises at a consistent rate, a country's own money supply must also grow. In addition to commodity movements, Locke advances his theory of foreign exchanges, stating that there are also movements in the country's stock of money, and that capital movements impact exchange rates. He finds the latter to be less important and volatile than commodity fluctuations. When it comes to a country's money stock, he claims that if it is high in comparison to other countries', it will cause the country's exchange rate to increase above par, just as an export balance would.

He also generates cash requirements estimates for various economic groupings, such as landowners, laborers, and brokers. He claims that the cash requirements in each group are inversely proportional to the length of the pay period. He claims that the brokers, whose activities widen the monetary circuit and whose profits eat into the wages of laborers and landowners, have a negative impact on both the personal and public economies to which they ostensibly contribute.

Ideas on the 'Self'

Locke expresses the self as "that conscious thinking thing, whatever substance, made up of whether spiritual, or material, simple, or compounded, it matters not, which is sensible, or conscious of pleasure and pain, capable of happiness or misery, and so is concerned for itself, as far as that consciousness extends." However, he does not disregard "substance", as he wrote, *"The body too goes to the making the man."*

Locke outlines the gradual unfolding of this conscious mind in his essay. Locke proposes the idea of an empty mind that is shaped by experience; sensations and reflections are the two sources of all of our ideas, arguing against both the Augustinian view of man as originally sinful and the Cartesian position, which holds that man innately knows basic logical propositions. He expresses himself in 'An Essay Concerning Human Understanding', *"This source of ideas every man has wholly within himself; and though it be not sense, as having nothing to do with external objects, yet it is very like it, and might properly enough be called internal sense."*

The blueprint of how to teach this mind can be found in John Locke's 'Some Thoughts Concerning Education.' He conveys the notion that education produces the man or, more fundamentally, that the mind is an "empty cupboard" in letters addressed to Mary Clarke and her husband concerning their son. He writes, "I think I may say that of all the men we meet with, nine parts of ten are what they are, good or evil, useful or not, by their education."

"The small and nearly imperceptible impacts on our young infancies have extremely substantial and permanent consequences," Locke said. He claimed that the "associations of thoughts" formed while one is young are more essential than those formed later because they form the foundation of the self; they are, in other words, what marks the tabula rasa first. Locke advises against allowing "a foolish maid" to persuade a kid that "goblins and sprites" are associated with the night in his Essay, since *"darkness must ever thereafter bring with it those awful conceptions, and they shall be so joined, that he can no more bear the one than the other."*

As nearly every educational writer warned parents not to allow their children to develop negative associations, this theory became known as associationism. It influenced 18th-century thought, particularly educational theory, as nearly every educational writer warned parents not to allow their children to develop negative associations. With David Hartley's attempt to uncover a biological mechanism for associationism in his Observations on Man, it also contributed to the formation of psychology and other new sciences.

Religious Beliefs

Locke's political opinions have been attributed to his religious beliefs by certain scholars. Locke's theological journey began with Calvinist trinitarianism. But by the time he wrote the "Reflections" in 1695, he was espousing not only Socinian tolerance beliefs, but also Socinian Christology. Locke was accused of Socinianism, Arianism, or Deism because he was unsure about the subject of original sin at times. The belief that *"all Adam's Posterity are doomed to Eternal Infinite Punishment, for Adam's Transgression"* was *"little consonant with the Justice or Goodness of the Great and Infinite God,"* according to Locke. He did not, however, deny the existence of evil. Man had the ability to wage unjust wars and commit crimes. Criminals ought to be punished, even if it meant death. Whether his notion of a 'criminal' included specific acts of king and dukes had not been determined.

Locke was a staunch conservative when it came to the Bible. He maintained the notion of the Bible's linguistic inspiration. The miracles attested to the biblical message's divine origins. As he demonstrated in his 1695 essay "Reasonableness of Christianity," Locke was convinced that the entire content of the Bible was in harmony with human reason. Despite being a proponent of tolerance, Locke urged authorities not to accept atheism, believing that denying God's existence would weaken social order and lead to chaos. This ruled out any forms of atheistic philosophy, as well as all attempts to derive ethics and natural law from exclusively secular premises. The cosmological argument, in Locke's perspective, was valid and demonstrated God's existence. His political views were influenced by Protestant Christian beliefs. Additionally, Locke supported a sense of piety out of thanks to God for imparting reason to humanity.

Philosophy of Religion

The belief in creation was the foundation of Locke's understanding of man. Locke connected natural law with biblical revelation. The core elements of Locke's political theory were derived from biblical scriptures, particularly Genesis 1 and 2 (the Creation), the Golden Rule, Jesus' teachings, Paul's epistle, and the Decalogue; God protects a person's life, reputation, and property, according to the Decalogue.

The Bible also influenced Locke's thinking on liberty. Locke deduced essential human equality, including gender equality, from the Bible, which became the foundation of the Imago Dei theological doctrine. One of the ramifications of the principle of equality, according to Locke, was that all persons were formed equally free, necessitating the consent of the governed. Locke equated the English monarchy's control over the British people to Adam's divinely given rule over Eve in Genesis. However, even that divine rule was to be per the unwavering connect of Eve.

The American Declaration of Independence, inspired by Locke's philosophy, based human rights in part on the biblical belief in creation. The Declaration of Independence is based on Locke's belief that governments require the consent of the governed. Most certainly, the Whigs, of whom Locke closely associated with, were in no way in consent or compliance with King Charles II.

Library & Manuscripts

Throughout his life, Locke was an avid book collector and notetaker. Locke had collected a library of almost 3,000 books by the time he died in 1704; a substantial number of the times. Locke, unlike several of his contemporaries, took great care to categorize and preserve his collection, and his will outlined how his library would be divided after his death. Friend Lady Masham was given the option of choosing *"any four folios, eight quartos, and twenty books of less volume, which she shall chose out of the works in my Library,"* according to Locke's will. Locke also gifted six titles to Anthony Collins, his close friend, but he left the remainder of his collection to his cousin, Peter King, and Lady Masham's son, Francis Cudworth Masham.

When Francis Masham attained the age of "one and twenty years," he was promised half of Locke's library. The remainder of Locke's books, as well as his manuscripts, were given to his cousin King. The Masham section of Locke's library was scattered throughout the next two centuries. The manuscripts and volumes given to King, on the other hand, remained with his successors until the Bodleian Library in Oxford purchased the majority of the collection in 1947. Paul Mellon, a collector and philanthropist, uncovered a portion of the books Locke bequeathed to King in 1951. Mellon augmented his discovery with books from Locke's library that he purchased privately before donating his collection to the Bodleian in 1978. Scholars interested in Locke, his philosophy, information management systems, and the history of the book have found the Locke Room at the Bodleian to be a helpful resource.

Locke's library contained printed works that reflected his diverse academic pursuits as well as his movements throughout his life. During the 1670s and 1680s, Locke traveled frequently in France and the Netherlands, and he collected many works from the continent. Only half of the volumes in Locke's library were printed in England, with France and the Netherlands accounting for over 40%. These books deal with a wide range of topics. Theology, medicine, politics and law, and classical literature were the most popular categories in Locke's collection, according to John Harrison and Peter Laslett. More than 800 books from Locke's library are currently housed at the Bodleian Library. Locke's reproductions of books by numerous of the seventeenth century's most significant individuals are among them. These include the following:

- *"An address to Protestants of All Persuasions"*, Wm. Penn
- *"The World Encompassed"*, Sir Francis Drake
- *"A Discourse of Things Above Reason"*, Robert Boyle
- *"The History of the Royal-Society of London"*, Tho. Sprat

Many of these books still contain Locke's own signature and notes he took regarding the book and its subject matter.

The Bodleian Library has around 100 manuscripts related to Locke or written in his hand, in addition to the volumes he owned. These manuscripts, like the books in Locke's collection, show a wide range of interests and provide distinct insights into Locke's life and relationships. Letters to and from acquaintances including Peter King and Nicolas Toinard, as well as his journals for most of the years between 1675 and 1704, are among the manuscripts. Early drafts of Locke's writings, such as his Essay Concerning Human Understanding, are among the most important texts. The Bodleian also has a copy of Robert Boyle's General History of the Air, which is marked up with Locke's revisions and notes as he prepared Boyle's work for posthumous publication. Unpublished compositions can be found in other manuscripts. Some of Locke's opinions on the Glorious Revolution, which he addressed to his friend Edward Clarke but never published, are among them.

Locke's notes and commonplace books are one of the most extensive collections of manuscripts at the Bodleian. Locke was dubbed a "Master Note-taker" by scholar Richard Yeo, who says, *"Locke's systematic note-taking pervaded most parts of his life."* Locke claimed in an unpublished essay titled "Of Study" that a notebook should function as a "chest-of-drawers" for organizing information, providing "great benefit to the memory and methods to avoid confusion in our thoughts." Locke kept a number of journals and commonplace books, which he divided into categories. Some contain Locke's theological notes, while others have medical notes. Other notebooks combine numerous themes in one notebook but divide them into parts.

These commonplace books were highly personal and were intended for Locke's personal use rather than being available to a broad audience. Locke's notes are frequently shortened and contain a plethora of codes that he used to cross-reference material between notebooks. Locke also customized his notebooks by inventing his own indexing system based on a grid layout and Latin keywords. His indexes condensed words to their first letter and vowel, rather than recording whole words. As a result, the word "Epistle" is classed as "Ei." In 1686, Locke published his approach in French, and it was reissued in English posthumously in 1706.

Some of the volumes in Locke's Bodleian library are a mix of manuscript and print editions. Some of Locke's works were interleaved, which meant that blank sheets were inserted between the printed pages to allow for commentary. Locke's five volumes of the New Testament were interleaved and annotated in French, Greek, and Latin. Locke did the same thing with his copy of Thomas Hyde's Bodleian Library catalogue, which he used to make his own library catalogue.

Synopsis

All of John Locke's thoughts and beliefs, whether written down or not, provided a strong insight into his mind and the groundwork for his actions. His philosophies on religious tolerance, his principle that everyone was equal and independent in a natural condition, and his conviction that everyone had an inherent right to defend his own life, health, liberty, and belongings, no matter the actions required to do so or the consequences there of, lay a clear path for the need to remove any monarch whose laws and mandates opposed the very concepts of Locke and the Whig movement.

It needs to be restated that Locke was known as "The Father of Liberalism", a moral and political philosophy based on liberty, the consent of those being governed, and equality before the law. And by 1683, in Locke's mind and in the minds of those he associated with, these philosophies were not being adhered to by the current British monarchy and, in fact, in many instances, was commanding the opposite. Above all, Locke certainly maintained the idea of a revolutionary disruption in which monarchy could be replaced, by force or by sheet intimidation. This notion played a major role in the Rye House Plot.

CHAPTER 2:
KING CHARLES II

Preamble

The "House of Stuart", initially called "Stewart", was a Scottish, English, Irish, and later British royal house. The surname Fitz Alan is derived from the title of High Steward of Scotland, which was held by the family's forefather, Walter fitz Alan, around 1150 A.D. By the time his grandson Walter Stewart was born, the name Stewart and its variants had established themselves as a family name. Robert II, the first monarch of the Stewart line, reigned as king and queen of Scotland from 1371 to 1603 and of England and Great Britain from 1603 to 1714. Mary, Queen of Scots, was raised in France and adopted the French spelling of the Stuart surname.

James IV married Margaret Tudor in 1503, tying the royal families of Scotland and England together. In the Union of the Crowns, James IV's great-grandson, James VI of Scotland, succeeded to the thrones of England and Ireland as James I. Elizabeth I of England died without issue in 1603, and James IV's great-grandson, James VI of Scotland, succeeded to the thrones of England and Ireland as James I.

Except for the Commonwealth period between 1649 and 1660, the Stuarts ruled Britain and Ireland and its expanding kingdom until Queen Anne's death in 1714. King Charles II's mandate resulted in the "Restoration" of the Stuart monarchy in 1660. The term 'restoration' is also used to denote the period following the establishment of a new political settlement, which lasted several years. It is sometimes used to refer to King Charles II's whole reign (1660–1685) as well as James, his younger brother, James' brief rule, from 1685 to 1688.

Some members of Parliament, former republicans, and portions of the Protestant people of England, however, were concerned that King Charle's relationship with France under Louis XIV and other Catholic rulers of Europe was too tight. Anti-Catholic prejudice, which connected Roman Catholicism with absolute monarchy, was widespread, and the succession to the English throne drew special attention. While Charles and his brother were openly Anglicans, they were known to have Catholic sympathies. When Charle's brother, James, also known as James, Duke of York, was discovered to have converted to Roman Catholicism in 1673, these fears were verified.

The Exclusion Bill was tabled in the House of Commons in 1681, spurred by the opposition-invented "Popish Plot", which would have prevented James from succeeding to the throne. The Oxford Parliament was dissolved after Charles outmaneuvered his opponents. As a result, his opponents had no legal way to stop James from succeeding, and suspicions of plans and conspiracies abounded. Lord Melville, Lord Leven, and Lord Ashley, the leaders of the opposition to Charles's authority, escaped to Holland, where Ashley died soon after. Many prominent members of Parliament and noblemen from the "country party" became known as Whigs, a moniker that persisted. Lord Ashley, a founder of the Whig movement and a mentor to John Locke, had a significant influence on Locke's political theories, as we now know.

Introduction

From 1649 to 1651, Charles II was King of Scotland, and from the Restoration of the monarchy in 1660 until his death in 1685, he was King of Scotland, England, and Ireland. Charles is known as the 'Merry Monarch', a reference to the liveliness and hedonism of his court, and is considered one of the most popular English rulers.

Charles II of England, Scotland, and Ireland was the eldest son of Charles I of England, Scotland, and Ireland and Henrietta Maria of France. The Parliament of Scotland proclaimed Charles II king on February 5, 1649, following Charles I's execution at Whitehall on January 30, 1649, at the end of the English Civil War. However, England entered the English Interregnum, often known as the English Commonwealth, during which time Oliver Cromwell led the kingdom as a de facto republic.

On September 3, 1651, Cromwell defeated Charles II in the Battle of Worcester, and Charles fled to mainland Europe. Cromwell essentially ruled England, Scotland, and Ireland. For the following nine years, Charles lived in exile in France, the Dutch Republic, and the Spanish Netherlands. Following Cromwell's death in 1658, a political crisis ended in the monarchy being restored, and Charles was asked to return to Britain. On his 30th birthday, May 29, 1660, he was greeted with great adulation in London. All official documents after 1660 stated the regnal year as if he had succeeded his father as king in 1649.

The Clarendon Code was enacted by Charles' English parliament to strengthen the re-established Church of England's status. Despite his preference for a policy of religious tolerance, Charles agreed to the Clarendon Code. The Second Anglo-Dutch War was an important foreign policy issue during his early reign.

He signed the Treaty of Dover in 1670, forming an alliance with his cousin, King Louis XIV of France. Charles secretly pledged to convert to Catholicism at an indeterminate future date if Louis agreed to assist him in the Third Anglo-Dutch War and provide him a pension. With his 1672 Royal Declaration of Indulgence, Charles attempted to grant religious freedom to Catholics and Protestant dissenters, but the English Parliament persuaded him to revoke it. Regardless of the countermand, members of the Whig were furious, with Lord Ashley their biggest protester.

When it was proven that Charles's brother and intended heir, James, Duke of York, was Catholic, Titus Oates' accusations of a rumored "Popish Plot" (to be covered later) provoked the "Exclusion Crisis" in 1679. Of the "Crisis", three exclusion bills attempted to keep James, Duke of York, the King's brother and likely heir, off the thrones of England, Scotland, and Ireland because he was a Roman Catholic. None of them became legislation. However, two new political parties emerged as a result; the Tories and the Whigs. The Tories were against the exclusion, but the "Country Party," afterwards known as the Whigs, were in favor. While Parliament did not deliberate on James' exclusion during Charles' reign, it would come to a head only three years after he assumed the throne. The pro-exclusion Whig and anti-exclusion Tory parties arose as a result of the conflict. In 1681, Charles disbanded the English Parliament and reigned on his own until his death in 1685.

Early Life, Civil War & Exile

Charles II was born at St James's Palace on May 29, 1630. Charles I, who governed the three kingdoms of England, Scotland, and Ireland, and Henrietta Maria, the French monarch Louis XIII's sister, were his parents. Their second child, Charles, was born to them. Their first son was born a year before Charles, but he died within a day of his birth. England, Scotland, and Ireland were

26

primarily Anglican, Presbyterian, and Catholic, respectively. On June 27, the Anglican Bishop of London, William Laud, baptized Charles at the Chapel Royal. He was raised by the Protestant Countess of Dorset, despite the fact that his godparents were Catholics: his maternal uncle Louis XIII and his maternal grandmother, Marie de' Medici, the Dowager Queen of France. Charles was born with the titles of Duke of Cornwall and Duke of Rothesay, as well as various more titles. He was named Prince of Wales around his seventh birthday; however, he was never properly invested.

During the English Civil War in the 1640s, when Charles was still a child, his father fought Parliamentary and Puritan forces. Charles was present at the Battle of Edgehill with his father, and at the age of fourteen, he took part in the wars of 1645, when he was named titular commander of the English forces in the West Country. By spring 1646, his father's campaign was losing, and Charles fled England for his own safety. After leaving Pendennis Castle, he traveled to the Isles of Scilly, Jersey, and eventually France, where his mother was already exiled and his first cousin, Louis XIV, was king. In May 1646, Charles I surrendered to his captors.

During the Second English Civil War, Charles moved to The Hague, where his sister Mary and brother-in-law William II, Prince of Orange, were more likely than his mother's French kin to lend major aid to the royalist cause. However, the royalist fleet that fell under Charles' authority was not put to any good use, and it did not arrive in Scotland in time to link up with the Duke of Hamilton's royalist Engager army before it was crushed by the Parliamentarians at the Battle of Preston.

Charles had a brief affair with Lucy Walter at The Hague, who afterwards claimed they had secretly married. One of Charles' many illegitimate children, James Crofts, subsequently known as James Scott and known as the 1st Duke of Monmouth and Duke of Buccleuch, was one of the most distinguished members of British society. Whether legitimate or not, James was Charles II's firstborn son. As James Scott is a major player in the Rye House Plot, he will be discussed in detail later.

King Charles I was beheaded in January 1649, despite his son's diplomatic efforts to preserve him, and England became a republic. At the Mercat Cross in Edinburgh, the Covenanter Parliament of Scotland named Charles II "King of Great Britain, France, and

Ireland," but would let him enter Scotland unless he agreed to the imposition of Presbyterianism throughout Britain and Ireland.

When discussions with the Scots came to a halt, Charles sent General Montrose to the Orkney Islands with a small army to threaten the Scots with invasion in the hopes of achieving a more favorable arrangement. Montrose was afraid that Charles would accept a compromise, so he invaded Scotland's mainland, nevertheless. He was apprehended and put to death. Charles grudgingly consented to uphold the provisions of a treaty reached at Breda between him and the Scottish Parliament, as well as the Solemn League and Covenant, which established Presbyterian church authority across the United Kingdom. He publicly agreed to the Covenant upon his arrival in Scotland on June 23, 1650. Although his rejection of Episcopal church government won him favor in Scotland, it made him unpopular in England. The Covenanters' "villainy" and "hypocrisy" grew on Charles, who despised them.

The Covenanters were defeated at the Battle of Dunbar on September 3, 1650, by a far smaller force headed by Oliver Cromwell. The Scots forces were split between royalist Engagers and Presbyterian Covenanters, who fought one another. Disillusioned by the Covenanters, Charles attempted to flee them in October by riding north to join an Engager force, an action that became known as "the Start," but the Presbyterians caught up with him and recovered him within two days. Nonetheless, the Scots remained Charles' best hope for restoration, and on January 1, 1651, he was anointed King of Scotland at Scone Abbey. It was determined to attack England because Cromwell's armies were endangering Charles' position in Scotland. The invasion was defeated at the Battle of Worcester on September 3, 1651, with many Scots refusing to participate, including Lord Argyll and other leading Covenanters, and few English royalists joining the force as it moved south into England.

Charles eluded capture by hiding in the Royal Oak at Boscobel House. Despite a £1,000 reward on his head, the risk of death for anyone caught helping him, and the difficulty in disguising Charles, who stood over six feet tall at the time, Charles managed to flee England in disguise, landing in Normandy on October 16, despite a reward of £1,000 on his head, the risk of death for anyone caught helping him, and the difficulty in disguising Charles, who stood over six feet tall at the time.

Cromwell was appointed Lord Protector of England, Scotland, and Ireland in 1653, under the Instrument of Government enacted by Parliament, thus putting the British Isles under military control. Charles enjoyed a life of leisure in Saint-Germain-en-Laye, near Paris, on a monthly payment of 600 'livres' from Louis XIV. Charles lacked the financial and political resources to mount a serious challenge to Cromwell's rule. Despite the Stuart family's connections to the Dutch Republic through Henrietta Maria and the Princess of Orange, France and the Dutch Republic joined Cromwell's administration in 1654, compelling Charles to flee France and seek aid from Spain, which dominated the Southern Netherlands at the time.

In 1656, Charles signed the Treaty of Brussels with Spain. In exchange for Charles' commitment to the battle against France, this attracted Spanish support for a restoration. The basis of the post-Restoration army was established by a motley army raised by Charles from his exiled countrymen. This small, underfunded, poorly equipped, and ill-disciplined force was the nucleus of the post-Restoration army. In 1657, the Commonwealth and France signed the Treaty of Paris, committing themselves to fighting Spain in the Netherlands. The Spanish force was led by Charles' younger brother James, Duke of York, who was a staunch Royalist. Charles's army of roughly 2,000 men met with Commonwealth troops battling the French at the Battle of the Dunes in 1658, as part of a larger Spanish force. By the end of the conflict, Charles' force had dwindled to around 1,000 men, and the chance of a Royalist mission to England was vanished with the English taking Dunkirk.

Restoration

After Cromwell's death in 1658, Charles' chances of recovering the throne appeared to be slim; Cromwell's son, Richard, succeeded him as Lord Protector. The new Lord Protector, on the other hand, had no prior experience in either military or civil administration. The Rump Parliament was brought back in 1659, and Richard resigned. The Governor of Scotland, George Monck, was fearful that the country would plunge into disorder during the civil and military upheaval that followed. Monck and his troops marched into London, forcing the Rump Parliament to accept members of the Long Parliament who had been expelled during Pride's Purge in December 1648. For the first time in nearly 20 years, the Long Parliament was dissolved, and a general election was held. The previous Parliament established the electoral requirements in order to restore a Presbyterian majority.

The limitations against royalist candidates and voters were extensively disregarded, and the elections produced a House of Commons that was fairly evenly divided on political and religious lines between Royalists and Parliamentarians. The new so-called Convention Parliament convened on April 25, 1660, and soon after approved Charles' vow of leniency and tolerance in the Declaration of Breda. Conscience would be free, and Anglican church policy would not be punitive. He would not expatriate or seize the assets of former opponents. Except for the regicides, practically all of his opponents would be pardoned. Above all, Charles stated that he will rule in concert with Parliament. The English Parliament declared Charles King and invited him to return, sending a message to Charles in Breda on May 8, 1660. A convention had been convened earlier in the year in Ireland, and Charles had already been pronounced the winner. In Dublin, he was declared king on May 14.

He left Scheveningen for England on May 25, 1660, arrived in Dover on May 25, 1660, and arrived in London on May 29, 1660, his 30th birthday. In the Act of Indemnity and Oblivion, Charles and Parliament extended amnesty to practically all of Cromwell's allies, although 50 persons were specifically excluded. In the end, nine regicides were put to death. They were hung, drawn, and quartered; others were sentenced to life in jail or just barred from holding public office for the rest of their lives. Posthumous decapitations were performed on the bodies of Oliver Cromwell, Henry Ireton, and John Bradshaw.

The English Parliament handed him a £1.2 million annual salary to manage the government, mostly from customs and excise duties. However, for the most of Charles' reign, the grant was insufficient. The actual revenue was, for the most part, substantially lower, leading to measures at court to save money by lowering the size and expenses of the royal household and raising money through unpopular inventions like the hearth tax.

The deaths of his youngest brother, Henry, and sister, Mary, from smallpox in the second half of 1660 tempered Charles' elation at the

Restoration. Around the same time, Anne Hyde, the daughter of Lord Chancellor Edward Hyde, claimed that she was expecting a child with Charles' brother, James, whom she had secretly married. Edward Hyde, who had been unaware of the marriage or pregnancy, was made Earl of Clarendon, bolstering his position as Charles' favorite minister.

Clarendon Code

The Convention Parliament was dissolved in December 1660, and the second English Parliament of the reign convened immediately after the crowning. The Cavalier Parliament was dominated by Royalists and Anglicans. It passed various acts to ensure Anglican dominance by discouraging non-conformity to the Church of England. The following were their names:

- Municipal officeholders were required to swear allegiance under the Corporation Act of 1661.
- The Anglican Book of Common Prayer was made mandatory by the Act of Uniformity of 1662.
- Except under the auspices of the Church of England, the Conventicle Act of 1664 forbade religious assemblies of more than five people.
- Exiled non-conforming pastors were barred from going within five miles of a parish from which they had been expelled under the Five Mile Act of 1665.

For the rest of Charles' reign, the Conventicle and Five Mile Acts remained in force. Even though Lord Clarendon was not directly responsible for these Acts and even protested against the Five Mile Act, they became known as the "Clarendon Code."

Social change accompanied the Restoration. Puritanism's popularity waned. Theatres reopened after being closed during Oliver Cromwell's reign, and bawdy "Restoration comedy" became a well-known genre. Restoration literature hailed or responded to the restored court, which included libertines like John Wilmot, 2nd Earl of Rochester, and theatre licenses granted by Charles demanded that female parts be played by "their natural actors," rather than by boys, as was often the practice before. Of Charles II, Wilmot said:

"We have a pretty, witty king,
Whose word no man relies on,
He never said a foolish thing,
And never did a wise one"

In response, Charles is alleged to have replied, *"That the matter was easily accounted for: For that his discourse was his own, his actions were the ministry's."*

The Great Plague & The Great Fire

In 1665, Charles had a serious health problem. It was the last major outbreak of the bubonic plague in England, and it was known as the Great Plague of London. In the week of September 17, the death toll peaked at 7,000 per week. In July, as Parliament gathered in Oxford, Charles, his family, and court departed London for Salisbury. Over the winter, the plague cases subsided, and Charles returned to London in February 1666.

On September 2, 1666, after a long period of hot and dry weather through mid-1666, another disaster, subsequently known as the Great Fire of London, began. On Pudding Lane, a fire broke out at a bakehouse. The fire, which was fanned by a strong easterly wind and fueled by wood and fuel inventories stored for the impending colder months, finally burnt over 13,200 homes and 87 churches, including St Paul's Cathedral. Charles and his brother, James, joined the firefighting operation and were in charge of it. The people accused Catholic conspirators for the fire, and one Frenchman, Robert Hubert, was hung based on a fake confession, despite the fact that he had nothing to do with it. IT would seem that the year 1666 (note the 666) was not a good era during Charles II's reign!

Foreign Policy & Marriage

Portugal had been at war with Spain since 1640, trying to reclaim its independence after a sixty-year dynastic union between the crowns of Spain and Portugal. France had previously aided Portugal, but in the Treaty of the Pyrenees of 1659, France abandoned Portugal. During his father's reign, discussions with Portugal for Charles II' marriage to Catherine of Braganza began, and after the restoration, Queen Lusa of Portugal, serving as regent, renewed negotiations with England, resulting in an alliance. A marriage pact was concluded on June 23, 1661. With trading privileges in Brazil and the East Indies, religious and commercial freedom in Portugal, and two million Portuguese crowns, England received Catherine's dowry of Tangier and the Seven Islands of Bombay. Portugal, on the other hand, gained military and naval backing against Spain, as well as Catherine's religious freedom. Catherine arrived in Portsmouth from Portugal on May 13, 1662, but Charles did not pay her a visit until May 20. The following day, the couple married in two ceremonies in Portsmouth. One was a private Catholic ceremony, and the other was a public Anglican service.

In the same year, Charles sold Dunkirk to his first cousin, King Louis XIV of France, for around £375,000. Although a valuable strategic outpost, the channel port was a drain on Charles's limited funds and his opposition was once again infuriated.

The Navigation Acts of 1650, which gave English warships a monopoly and sparked the First Dutch War, which lasted from 1652 to 1654, had harmed Dutch trade and sparked the First Dutch War. In November 1660, envoys from the States General arrived with the Dutch Gift to lay the groundwork for a fresh beginning. English attempts to encroach on Dutch colonies in Africa and North America sparked the Second Dutch War, which lasted from 1665 to 1667. With the conquest of New Amsterdam and a win at the Battle of Lowestoft, the English had a good start in the war. In honor of Charles's brother James, Duke of York, New Amsterdam was renamed "New York." The Dutch, on the other hand, surprised England in 1667 when they sailed up the River Thames to where a large portion of the English fleet was docked. Except for the flagship, Royal Charles, which was brought back to the Netherlands as a prize, almost all of the ships were sunk. The Treaty of Breda brought the Second Dutch War to a close.

Following the Second Dutch War, Charles fired Lord Clarendon, whom he had used as a scapegoat for the conflict. When Clarendon was impeached for high treason, which carried the death penalty, he escaped to France. The Cabal, a witty acronym for a group of five politicians, was given power. Clifford, Arlington, Buckingham, Ashley, and Lauderdale were their names. In actuality, the Cabal rarely worked together, and the court was frequently split between two factions led by Arlington and Buckingham, with Arlington having the upper hand.

In the War of Devolution, England joined forces with Sweden and its erstwhile foe, the Netherlands, to confront Louis XIV. Although Louis reached an agreement with the Triple Alliance, he maintained his aggressive intentions toward the Netherlands. In 1670, Charles agreed to the Treaty of Dover, under which Louis XIV would pay him £160,000 per year to ease his financial problems. In exchange, Charles vowed to provide troops to Louis and announce his conversion to Catholicism "as soon as the welfare of his kingdom will allow." To crush those who opposed the conversion, Louis was to provide him with 6,000 men. Charles worked hard to keep the Treaty, particularly the conversion clause, hidden, though unsuccessfully, leading to further resentment from opposition groups like the Whigs.

Meanwhile, Charles granted the East India Company the right to govern its territorial acquisitions autonomously, mint money, command fortresses and troops, form alliances, make war and peace, and exercise both civil and criminal jurisdiction over its possessions in the Indies through a series of five charters. He had already leased the Bombay islands to the business for a minimal price of £10 paid in gold in 1668. The Portuguese lands Catherine received as a dowry proved too costly to preserve, and Tangier was abandoned in 1684. By royal charter in 1670, Charles gave the Hudson's Bay Company authority of the whole Hudson Bay drainage basin, naming the province Rupert's Land after his cousin Prince Rupert of the Rhine, the company's first governor.

Conflict with Parliament

The Cavalier Parliament, which had previously been supportive of the Crown, was alienated by the king's wars and religious policies in the 1670s. In 1672, Charles published the Royal Declaration of Indulgence, claiming that all punitive laws against Catholics and other religious dissenters would be suspended. He openly supported Catholic France in the same year, and the Third Anglo-Dutch War began. This conflict with Parliament was well known among the opposition, which further fueled the fires of antagonism.

On constitutional grounds, the Cavalier Parliament opposed the "Declaration of Indulgence", stating that the king had the jurisdiction to suspend legislation approved by Parliament at will. Charles retracted the Declaration and agreed to the Test Act, which obliged public officers to not only receive the sacrament in the Church of England's authorized forms, but also to repudiate transubstantiation and the Catholic Mass as "superstitious and idolatrous" afterwards. Clifford, who had converted to Catholicism, refused to take the pledge and died soon after, possibly by suicide, though murder by the Whig resistance had not been ruled out. England had achieved nothing from the Anglo-Dutch War by 1674, and the Cavalier Parliament refused to grant additional finances, pushing Charles to make peace. The Cabal's dominance diminished, while Lord Danby, Clifford's replacement, expanded.

Queen Catherine, Charles II's wife, was unable to bear an heir. Her four pregnancies in 1662, February 1666, May 1668, and June 1669 all ended in miscarriages and stillbirths. As a result, James, Duke of York, Charles's detested Catholic brother, was the apparent successor. This probable outcome did not sit well with the Whigs, prompting Lord Ashley to facilitate meetings among his assemblage.

Charles then decided that James's daughter, Mary, should marry the Protestant William of Orange, partly to allay public misgivings that the royal family was 'overly' Catholic. Titus Oates, an Anglican and Jesuit priest who alternated between the two, erroneously warned of a "Popish Plot" to assassinate Charles in 1678, even accusing the queen of collaboration. In order to provide additional detail given the importance of this event, the Popish Plot was a false conspiracy concocted by Titus Oates that engulfed the Kingdoms of England and Scotland in anti-Catholic panic between 1678 and 1681. Oates claimed there was a large-scale Catholic plot to assassinate Charles II. Although Charles did not accept the accusations, he did instruct his senior minister, Lord Danby, to look into them. While Danby appears to have been doubtful of Oates' assertions, the Cavalier Parliament believed them. Anti-Catholic frenzy gripped the population. Whether the Popish Plot was fictional or not, alleged conspirators were round up and found guilty by judges and juries around the country. This led to the hanging of at least 22 innocent individuals, including Oliver Plunkett, the Catholic Archbishop of Armaghwhich. Oates' complex web of claims eventually unraveled, leading to his arrest and conviction for perjury.

Between 1678 and 1681, the Society of Jesus suffered the most. Nine Jesuits were executed and twelve died in jail at this time. Three more people died as a result of the panic. They also lost Combe, which was the Jesuit headquarters for South Wales, in Herefordshire. The struggle of the Jesuits during this time period is shown by a remark from French Jesuit Claude de la Colombière. "The name of the Jesuit is loathed beyond all else, even by secular and regular priests, as well as by the Catholic people, because it is thought that the Jesuits have generated this roaring storm, which is likely to topple the entire Catholic religion," he says.

The hysteria also impacted other Catholic religious orders such as the Carmelites, Franciscans, and Benedictines. Within England, they were no longer allowed to have more than a set number of members or missions. According to John Kenyon, European religious organizations all over the continent were harmed because many of them relied on the donations of the English Catholic community to survive. Because the Privy Council intended to make sure that everyone who could have information about the alleged plot was apprehended and tried, a large number of Catholic priests were imprisoned and tried.

The panic had major ramifications for both ordinary Catholics and priests in the United Kingdom. A proclamation was issued on October 30, 1678, requiring any Catholics who were not craftsmen or property owners to leave London and Westminster. They were not allowed to travel inside a 12-mile radius of the city unless they had special permission. Catholics were subjected to fines, harassment, and incarceration throughout this time.

Danby was impeached by the House of Commons in 1678 and charged with high treason. Despite the fact that majority of the country wanted to fight Catholic France, Charles had secretly met with Louis XIV to try to make an agreement in which England would remain neutral in exchange for money. Danby had declared openly that he was anti-French, but he had decided to follow by Charles's demands. Unfortunately for him, the House of Commons did not see him as a willing participant in the scandal, assuming instead that he was the policy's originator. In January 1679, Charles dissolved the Cavalier Parliament to save Danby from an impeachment trial.

The new English Parliament, which convened in March of that year, was staunchly opposed to Charles II. Many people thought he was planning to deploy the standing army to repress dissent or impose Catholicism. However, due to a lack of funding approved by

Parliament, Charles was compelled to dismantle his army gradually. Danby resigned as Lord High Treasurer after losing Parliament's backing, but the monarch granted him a pardon. The House of Commons declared, against the royal will, that the dissolution of Parliament did not halt impeachment proceedings, and that the pardon was thus unlawful. The impeachment became stuck between the two Houses when the House of Lords attempted to impose the sentence of exile. Charles yielded to the requests of his opponents, committing Danby to the Tower of London, where he was kept for another five years, as he had done so many times during his reign.

Both the Declaration of Indulgence and the Popish Plot were the last straws as far as the opposition was concerned. The need for the removal of King Charles II and heir to the throne, James, Duke of York, was now blatantly apparent to all opposition parties, including Lord Ashley.

Charles II & Science

William Cavendish, Earl of Newcastle, was the superintendent of the royal household during Charles II's childhood, and Brian Duppa, Dean of Christchurch, was his tutor. Neither man considered it was proper for a future king to study science topics, and Newcastle even warned against taking any subject too seriously. However, when Charles grew older, he was tutored by renowned physician William Harvey. He was well-known for his work on blood circulation in the human body and already served as Charles I's physician; his research influenced Charles's attitude toward science. Harvey accompanied Charles I to the Battle of Edgehill as the king's senior physician. He was given command of the two princes, Charles and his brother James, in the morning, but the boys returned to their father for the opening of the war.

Charles completed his education in exile, studying physics, chemistry, and navigational mathematics. His Latin and Greek professors were the clergyman John Earle, best known for his satirical book "Microcosmographie", and Thomas Hobbes, the philosopher and author of "Leviathon", with whom he studied mathematics. Even though part of his studies and experiments were merely to pass the time, by the time Charles returned to England, he had already mastered navigational mathematics and was a capable chemist. Charles was enthralled by the new ideas and discoveries that were being made at the time. He had a sundial and a 35-foot-long telescope installed in the Privy garden soon after his coronation.

A group of scientists began meeting informally in the 1640s at Wadham College in Oxford or Gresham College in London. Free weekly lectures on a range of topics were already being delivered at Gresham College at the time, and the new group wanted to take a more academic and educated approach to science, as well as undertake experiments in physics and mathematics. Harvey, Christopher Wren, Robert Hooke, and Robert Boyle were among the members of this group. Almost all activities ended during the civil war, but after the Restoration in November 1668, Wren presented a lecture, following which a society was formed. It began with 12 members, but by the end of the year, it had grown to 41. In 1662, Charles was already familiar with members of the new society or was aware of their activities, and he immediately consented to give them royal sanction as the Royal Society. Following the charter's approval, the organization became more formalized, with members paying a ten-shilling election fee and a shilling each week for meetings, whether they were present or not. Hooke was named Curator of Experiments in November. Hooke conducted frequent demonstrations of experiments with the support of a laboratory assistant, and this was a salaried position. Charles was aware of Hooke's weekly rallies and threatened to appear in person in July 1663, much to the Society's dismay. Wren was approached for guidance in order to guarantee that the presentation was suitable for the monarch. In the end, neither Charles nor his cousin Prince Rupert paid a visit to the society.

Charles grew disinterested in the society's operations over time and left it to its own ways, but he continued to support scientific and commercial projects. In 1673, he established the Mathematical School at Christ's Hospital, and two years later, he established the Royal Observatory at Greenwich in response to concerns about French progress in astronomy. He kept his passion in chemistry alive by setting up a laboratory beneath the Privy Gallery. Dissections were periodically performed there, and the king was present to see them. On the morning of Friday, 15 January 1669, while walking to Whitehall, Samuel Pepys met the king, who asked him to see his science laboratory, according to his diary. Pepys' scientific understanding was limited, and he admitted that what he saw there was beyond his comprehension.

Later in life, Charles had excruciating gout, which reduced the daily walks he used to take on a regular basis when he was younger. His zeal was now focused into his laboratory, where he would spend hours upon hours working on his research. Charles developed a fascination with mercury and would spend entire mornings trying to distill it. Unfortunately, heating mercury in an open crucible produces toxic mercury vapor, which may have contributed to his eventual health problems.

Because his Catholic brother James was next in line to the throne, Charles faced a political maelstrom. Lord Ashley, now the 1st Earl of Shaftesbury, was a staunch opponent of a Catholic monarchy. The House of Commons introduced the Exclusion Bill in 1679, which intended to remove the Duke of York from the line of succession, bolstering Ashley's power base. Some even attempted to bestow the throne on the Protestant Duke of Monmouth, Charles's illegitimate son. The Abhorrers, who were opposed to the Exclusion Bill, were dubbed "Tories" after a nickname for dispossessed Irish Catholic robbers. Meanwhile, supporters of a petitioning campaign in favor of the Exclusion Bill were dubbed "Whigs," a derogatory word for rebellious Scottish Presbyterians.

The Absolute Monarch

Fearing that the Exclusion Bill would pass, and bolstered by acquittals in the ongoing Plot trials, which he saw as indicating a more favorable public mood toward Catholicism, Charles II dismissed the English Parliament for the second time that year, in mid-1679. Charles' aspirations for a more moderate Parliament were dashed, and he disbanded Parliament once more after it attempted to enact the Exclusion Bill.

In March 1681, when a new Parliament convened at Oxford, Charles II dissolved it for the fourth time after only a few days. During the 1680s, however, public support for the Exclusion Bill waned, and Charles' popularity soared across the country.

The so-called "Tory Reaction" began with the end of the Oxford Parliament. Lord Ashley, Earl of Shaftesbury, John Locke's tutor and sponsor, was imprisoned on suspicion of high treason and sent to the Tower of London on July 2, 1681. He filed a writ of habeas corpus with the Old Bailey right away, but the Old Bailey stated it didn't have authority over convicts in the Tower of London. As a result,

Ashley had to wait until the following Court of King's Bench session. On October 24, 1681, Shaftesbury applied for a writ of habeas corpus. On November 24, 1681, his case was ultimately heard by a grand jury.

Lord Ashley's case against the government was exceptionally weak. The government recognized that the majority of the witnesses used against him had already perjured themselves, and the documentary evidence was inconclusive. This, combined with the fact that the jury was hand-picked by the Whig Sheriff of London, meant the government had a slim chance of succeeding. The action against Lord Ashley was dismissed on February 13, 1682. Crowds in London chanted *"No Popish Successor, No York, A Monmouth"* and *"God bless the Earl of Shaftesbury"* in response to the announcement. Of course, their demands referred to the removal of James, Duke of York, as heir to the throne, with their plead for "A Monmouth", referring to the eventual crowning of James Scott, 1st Earl of Monmouth.

In May 1682, Charles II fell ill, and Lord Ashley convened a group to determine what to do if the king died. The group included John Locke, James Scott, Ford Grey the 3rd Baron Grey of Werke, Sir Thomas Armstrong, and Ashley's close political ally, Lord William Russell. The result of the meeting was to launch an insurgence demanding the establishment of a new parliament to settle the question of succession to the throne. Much to the dismay of Ashley and the others, Charles II recovered and need for a rebellion was deemed not necessary . . . at least not at this time.

The Tory party candidates won the election of the Sheriffs of London in July 1682. Lord Ashley was concerned that these Sheriffs would be able to appoint Tory sympathizers to juries, and he feared that he would be prosecuted for high treason once more. As a result, Ashley began conversations with the same group about staging synchronized rebellions around the country. Ashley was considerably more eager for a violent revolt than the others, and the uprising was repeatedly postponed, much to Ashley's dismay.

Lord Ashley became anxious after the new Tory sheriffs were installed on September 28, 1682. He continued to call for a quick rebellion and met with John Wildman to explore the possibilities of assassinating the king and Duke of York. These discussions most certainly took place in front of John Locke who, obviously, did nothing to prevent or discourage them.

With his plots unsuccessful, Lord Ashley decided to flee the country. He landed at the historic seaport of Brielle in the western Netherlands sometime between November 20 and 26, 1682. He then reached Rotterdam on November 28, and finally arrived in Amsterdam on December 2, 1682.

Lord Ashley's health had deteriorated considerably during this voyage. He fell ill In Amsterdam, and by the end of December he found it difficult to keep down any food. He drew up his will on January 17, 1683. On January 20, in a conversation with Robert Ferguson who had accompanied him to Amsterdam, he professed himself an Arian; a religious belief that the Son of God did not always exist, but was created within time by God the Father. Ashley died the following day at the age of 61.

According to the provisions of his will, Lord Ashley's body was shipped back to Dorset on February 13, 1683. He was buried at Wimborne St Giles on February 26. Ashley's passing left John Locke devastated, blaming the monarchy and others for his illness brought on by stress, trauma, and potential poisoning, though that scenario was highly unlikely.

Offspring

Charles II had no legal offspring, but seven mistresses acknowledged a dozen, including five by Barbara Villiers, also known as Lady Castlemaine, for whom the Dukedom of Cleveland was established. Moll Davis, Nell Gwyn, Elizabeth Killigrew, Catherine Pegge, Lucy Walter, and Louise de Kérouaille, the Duchess of Portsmouth, were among his numerous mistresses. As a result, he was known as "Old Rowley" during his lifetime, after his favorite racehorse, who was also a stallion.

His subjects despised paying taxes to support his mistresses and their children, many of whom were granted dukedoms or earldoms. The current Dukes of Buccleuch, Richmond, Grafton, and St. Albans are all male descendants of Charles. Diana, Princess of Wales, was descended from the Dukes of Grafton and Richmond, two of Charles's illegitimate offspring. Prince William, Duke of Cambridge, Diana's son and the second in line to the British throne, is expected to be the first king descended from Charles II.

Charles's eldest son was James Scott, the 1st Duke of Monmouth, whose mother was Charle's mistress, Lucy Walter. Of all King

Charles II's children, James Scott was the only one to attain political interest and accomplishments of any kind. Although strikingly handsome with the outward bearing of an ideal monarch, he lacked the intelligence and resolution required for the position of king, much less the struggle of power. And being one of the main architects of the Rye House Plot, the only one with a personal and kin association in the conspiracy, his background, mindset and motivation is the next to be explored.

CHAPTER 3:
JAMES, DUKE
OF YORK

Introduction

From February 6, 1685, until his deposition in the Glorious Revolution of 1688, James II and VII reigned as King of England and Ireland as James II and King of Scotland as James VII. He was England's, Scotland's, and Ireland's last Catholic ruler. His reign is currently mostly noted for battles over religious tolerance. However, it also encompassed the notions of absolutism and divine right of monarchs, and his overthrow confirmed Parliament's primacy over the Crown, putting an end to a century of political and civil strife.

With widespread support in all three nations, James inherited the thrones of England, Ireland, and Scotland from his elder brother Charles II, mostly based on the notions of divine right or birth. When the English and Scottish Parliaments refused to accept his measures, James attempted to impose them by decree; ultimately, it was a political principle, not a religious one, that led to his ouster.

Two occurrences in June 1688 pushed discontent into a catastrophe. The birth of James's son and successor James Francis Edward on June 10 threatened to establish a Roman Catholic dynasty, excluding his Anglican daughter Mary and her Protestant husband William III of Orange. The prosecution of the Seven Bishops for seditious libel was the second. This was seen as a direct attack on the Church of England, and their acquittal on June 30th effectively ended his political power in England. Anti-Catholic rioting in England and Scotland made it appear that only his abdication would avoid a civil war.

William of Orange was asked to take the English throne by leading members of the English political establishment. James' army fled after he landed at Brixham on November 5, 1688, and he went into exile in France on December 23. In February 1689, a special Parliament declared that the king had "vacated" the English throne and placed William and Mary as joint monarchs, establishing the notion that power came from Parliament rather than birth.

On March 14, 1689, James landed in Ireland in an attempt to reclaim his kingdoms, but despite a parallel uprising in Scotland, a Scottish Convention followed England's lead in April, concluding that James had "forfeited" the throne and offered it to William and Mary. After losing the Battle of the Boyne in July 1690, James retreated to France and spent the rest of his life in exile at Saint-Germain, where he was sheltered by Louis XIV. Although he was often depicted by his opponents as an absolute ruler, some historians have lauded him for preaching religious tolerance throughout the twentieth century, and more recent scholarship has attempted to establish a medium ground between both viewpoints.

Early Years

On October 14, 1633, King Charles I and his wife, Henrietta Maria of France, gave birth to their second son, James, at St James's Palace in London. He was born Duke of York, was given the Order of the Garter in 1642, and was legally created Duke of York in January 1644. He was baptized by William Laud, the Anglican Archbishop of Canterbury, later that year. Along with his older brother, the future King Charles II, and the Duke of Buckingham's two sons, George and Francis Villiers, he was taught by private tutors. James was made Lord High Admiral at the age of three; the title was first honorary, but during the Restoration, when James was an adult, it became a substantive appointment.

Civil War

The English Civil War erupted as a result of the King's disagreements with the English Parliament. James fought alongside his father at the Battle of Edgehill, narrowly avoiding capture by Parliamentary forces. He continued in Oxford after that, where he was conferred a Master of Arts by the University on November 1, 1642, and served as colonel of a voluntary foot regiment. Parliamentary leaders ordered the Duke of York to be imprisoned in St James's Palace when the city fell after the siege of Oxford in 1646. In 1648, the 14-year-old escaped from the Palace with the help of Joseph Bampfield and crossed the North Sea to The Hague, disguised as a woman.

When his father, Charles I, was assassinated by rebels in 1649, monarchists crowned his older brother, James, king. The Parliaments of Scotland and Ireland both accepted Charles II as king, and he was crowned at Scone in 1651. Despite being acclaimed king in Jersey, Charles was unable to obtain the English throne and escaped to exile in France.

Exile

James, like his brother, found sanctuary in France, where he served in Turenne's army against the Fronde and later against their Spanish allies. According to one witness, James received his first actual war experience in the French army, when *"he chances himself and chargeth gallantly where anything is to be done."* James was given command of a captured Irish regiment in December 1652, and was made Lieutenant-General in 1654, thanks to Turenne's favor.

Meanwhile, Charles attempted to retake his throne, but France, despite sheltering the exiles, had formed an alliance with Oliver Cromwell. In 1656, Charles appealed to Spain for help, despite the fact that Spain was an adversary of France, and an alliance was formed. As a result, James was compelled to abandon Turenne's army and was exiled from France.

James and his brother fought over Spain's diplomatic victory over France. Exiled and impoverished, neither Charles nor James could do much about the broader political situation, so James went to Bruges and joined the Spanish army in Flanders, where he was given command as Captain-General of six regiments of British volunteers and fought against his former French comrades at the Battle of the Dunes.

James became friendly with two Irish Catholic brothers in the Royalist retinue, Peter and Richard Talbot, during his service in the Spanish army, and grew estranged from his brother's Anglican counselors.

The French and Spanish made peace in 1659. James pondered accepting a Spanish invitation to serve as an admiral in their navy because he doubted his brother's chances of recovering the crown. He eventually declined the position; nevertheless, the situation in England had altered by the following year, and Charles II had been declared.

Restoration, Marriage & Politics

Charles II was restored to the English throne after the Commonwealth collapsed in 1660. Despite the fact that James was the apparent successor, it appeared improbable that he would succeed to the throne because Charles was still a young man capable of fathering children. Following his brother's restoration, James was made Duke of Albany in Scotland on December 31, 1660, in addition to his English title of Duke of York. When James returned to England, he caused a stir by announcing his engagement to Anne Hyde, the daughter of Charles's senior minister, Edward Hyde.

While attempting to attract Anne in 1659, James pledged to marry her. Anne got pregnant in 1660, but no one at the royal court anticipated a prince to marry a commoner after the Restoration and James's return to power, no matter what he had sworn prior. Despite the fact that practically everyone, including Anne's father, advised them not to marry, the pair wedded in secret and subsequently had an official wedding on September 3, 1660, in London.

Their first child, Charles, was born less than two months later, but he, like five other sons and girls, died in infancy. Only Mary, born on April 30, 1662, and Anne, born on February 6, 1665, survived. James was fond of his children and his job as a father, according to Samuel Pepys, and played with them "like an average private father of a kid," in contrast to the detached parenting practiced by royalty at the time.

James's wife was dedicated to him and played a significant role in his actions. Despite this, he had mistresses, notably Arabella Churchill and Catherine Sedley, and was known as *"his time's most unrestrained ogler."* James *"did eye my wife exceedingly,"* according to Samuel Pepys' journal. Gilbert Burnet famously remarked that James' girlfriends must have been "given him by his priests as a punishment," implying that James' mistresses must have been "given him by his priests as a penance." In 1671, Anne Hyde died.

Following the Restoration, James was confirmed as Lord High Admiral, a position that included the additional responsibilities of Governor of Portsmouth and Lord Warden of the Cinque Ports. In October 1660, Charles II appointed his brother as Governor of the Royal Adventurers into Africa, eventually shortened to the Royal African Company. James held the position until he was forced to retire during the Glorious Revolution. During the Second Anglo-

Dutch War, while James was in command of the Royal Navy, he promptly authorized the fleet to take forts off the African coast that would aid British involvement in the slave trade. Of course, British raids on forts occupied by the Dutch led to the outbreak of the war. During the Third Anglo-Dutch Wars, which included considerable warfare off the African coast, James remained Admiral of the Fleet. James directed the survey and re-fortification of the southern coast following the raid on the Medway in 1667. James had enough money to keep a large court household thanks to the job of Lord High Admiral and his revenue from post office and wine duties, which he received from his brother King Charles II.

James received American area between the Delaware and Connecticut rivers from Charles in 1664. Following its British conquest, the former Dutch colony of New Netherland and its main port, New Amsterdam, were given the names Province and City of New York in honor of James. The Duke gave part of the colony to entrepreneurs George Carteret and John Berkeley after it was founded. Fort Orange, on the Hudson River 150 miles north, was renamed Albany after James' Scottish title. He was appointed Governor of the Hudson's Bay Company in 1683, but he did not participate actively in its government.

In September 1666, in the absence of Lord Mayor Thomas Bloodworth, his brother Charles placed him in charge of firefighting operations during the Great Fire of London. Although this was not a political position, his acts and leadership were notable. In a letter dated September 8, a witness said, "The Duke of York hath won the hearts of the people with his incessant and untiring struggles day and night in endeavoring to quench the Fire."

James had been exposed to the ideas and ceremonies of the Roman Catholic Church throughout his time in France, as he and his wife, Anne, were drawn to that faith. James converted to Catholicism in 1668 or 1669, though he continued to attend Anglican services until 1676, keeping his conversion a secret for almost a decade. Despite his conversion, James maintained close ties with Anglicans such as John Churchill and George Legge, as well as French Protestants like Louis de Duras, Earl of Feversham.

In 1673, the English Parliament passed a new Test Act in response to growing concerns about Roman Catholic influence at court. All civil and military authorities were forced to take an oath under this Act, which included disavowal of the dogma of transubstantiation and denunciation of specific Roman Church activities as superstitious and idolatrous. The Eucharist was served to them under the auspices of the Church of England. James declined to carry out either action and instead chose to resign as Lord High Admiral. His conversion to Roman Catholicism became public as a result.

James' conversion was challenged by King Charles II, who ordered James' daughters, Mary and Anne, to be raised in the Church of England. Despite this, he let James to marry Mary of Modena, an Italian princess of fifteen years. On September 20, 1673, James and Mary were married by proxy in a Roman Catholic ceremony. On November 21, Mary came in England, and Bishop Nathaniel Crew of Oxford presided over a brief Anglican service that did little more than acknowledge the marriage by proxy. Many British citizens, who were suspicious of Catholicism, saw the new Duchess of York as a papist's emissary. James was known for his sincerity. *"If the occasion arose, I pray God would grant me his grace to suffer death as well as banishment for the real Catholic religion,"* he once declared.

Exclusion & Pre-Rye House Plot

King Charles II arranged for James' daughter Mary to marry Prince William III of Orange, the Protestant son of Charles and James' sister Mary, in 1677. After his brother and nephew agreed to the marriage, James grudgingly accepted. Despite the Protestant marriage, suspicions of a future Catholic monarch continued, heightened by Charles II's and Catherine of Braganza's inability to have children. Titus Oates, a defrocked Anglican clergyman, spoke of a "Popish Plot" to assassinate Charles and install the Duke of York on the throne. A wave of anti-Catholic frenzy swept the country as a result of the invented conspiracy.

Lord Ashley, Earl of Shaftesbury, a close supporter of John Locke and a former government minister who was now a strong opponent of Catholicism, presented an Exclusion Bill that would have removed James from the line of succession in England. Some members of Parliament even suggested that Charles's illegitimate son, James Scott, 1st Duke of Monmouth, should inherit the throne. With the Exclusion Bill in jeopardy, Charles II dissolved Parliament in 1679. In 1680 and 1681, two more Parliaments were elected, but both were dissolved for the same reason. The Exclusion Crisis aided in the formation of the English two-party system, with the Whigs supporting the Bill and the Tories opposing it. The succession was not changed in the end, but James was persuaded to withdraw from all policy-making committees and accept a smaller part in his brother's administration.

James departed England for Brussels on the King's orders. However, in 1680, he was named Lord High Commissioner of Scotland, and he moved to Edinburgh's Holyrood Palace to put down an insurrection and supervise royal government. When Charles became ill and appeared to be on the verge of death, James went to England. The accusations' fever subsided, but James' relationships with many in the English Parliament, including the Earl of Danby, a previous ally, were difficult for the rest of his life, and a sizable portion of the population turned against him. It would be another three years before Lord Ashley and James II's nephew, James Scott, would rally a murder plot against him and his brother, the King.

Portrait of Locke in 1697 at age 65, by Godfrey Kneller, the leading portrait painter in England during the late 17th and early 18th centuries. Locke was one of the greatest philosophers in Europe at the end of the 17th century. He grew up and lived through one of the most extraordinary centuries of English intellectual and political history. It was a century of conflicts between Crown and Parliament and the overlapping conflicts between Protestants, Anglicans and Catholics eventually swirled into Civil war. It was also marked by continued conflicts between the King and Parliament, and debates over religious toleration for Catholics and Protestant dissenters.

Anthony Ashley Cooper, also known as Lord Ashley and 1st Earl of Shaftesbury. Ashley, one of the richest men in England, came to Oxford in 1666 to drink medicinal waters, which by fate Locke delivered to him. As a result, Ashley invited Locke to move to London full time as his personal physician. Under Ashley, who became his mentor and patron, Locke was also his secretary, researcher, political operative, and good friend. However, he soon found himself at the very center of English politics and revolts in the 1670s and 1680s.

A N

E S S A Y

CONCERNING

𝕳umane 𝖀nderſtanding.

In Four BOOKS.

*Quam bellum eſt velle confiteri potius neſcire quod neſ-
cias, quam iſta effutientem nauſeare, atque ipſum ſibi
diſplicere !* Cic. de Natur. Deor. *l.* 1.

LONDON:

Printed for *Tho. Baſſet,* and ſold by *Edw. Mory*
at the Sign of the *Three Bibles* in St. *Paul's*
Church-Yard. M DC XC.

Locke's most famous work, published in 1689 but written earlier.

Charles II was King of Scotland from 1649 to 1651, then King of Scotland, England, and Ireland from the 1660 Restoration of the monarchy until his death in 1685. Charles II was the eldest surviving child of Charles I of England, Scotland and Ireland, and Henrietta Maria of France. He and his younger brother, James, Duke of York, were the target of numerous accusations, conspiracies, controversies and subversions in their day - but none like the Rye House Plot in 1683 whose consequences were far reaching.

James was King of England and Ireland as James II, and King of Scotland as James VII, from February 1685 upon the death of his brother, Charles II, until he was deposed in the Glorious Revolution of 1688. When he died at the age of 67, his heart was placed in a silver-gilt locket, his brain in a lead casket, his entrails in two gilt urns, and the flesh from his right arm was given to the English Augustinian nuns of Paris. The rest of his body was laid in a triple sarcophagus. During the French Revolution, his tomb was raided.

Portrait of James Scott, 1st Duke of Monmouth, a Dutch-born English nobleman. Originally called James Fitzroy or James Crofts, he was born in Rotterdam and was the eldest (illegitimate) son of Charles II and (one of) his mistress, Lucy Walter. James Scott and John Locke knew each other well enough for Locke to make arrangements for fellow conspirators in the plot to assassinate Scott's father, the King. Locke also networked with Scott to make arrangements for Phillip Locke, the 7th-Great Grandfather of this book's author, to immigrate to the English Colonies in America.

*The Rye House as it looked in 1683 at the time of the plot.
(Below) Rye House, as it looks today. Only the gate house remains.*

Late 17th-century composite engraving comprising seven portraits of figures of the Plot, all of whom were dead by 1685. They are Sir Thomas Armstrong, the Earl of Argyll, the Earl of Essex, Henry Cornish, William Russell, Lord Russell, James Scott, and Algernon Sidney, with one of Edmund Berry Godfrey whose unexplained death triggered the Popish Plot allegations against Catholics.

17th century engravings depicting the Rye House Plot.

17th century images of the results and consequences of the Plot conspirators, including being hanged, drawn & quartered (above) and burned at the stake (below), punishment for the only female deemed guilty by the court, Elizabeth Gaunt. Of the 40 found guilty and/or suspected of treason, nearly half managed to escape death and imprisonment. The actual guilt of most remains questionable.

Graphic of Arthur Capell, the 1st Earl of Essex, cutting his own throat within the Tower of London, rather than facing future consequences for his apparent role in the Plot.

The death of Charles II as depicted in this early drawing. Brother, James was heir to the throne, thereby becoming King James II.

The "Glorious Revolution of 1688" was the deposition of James II, King of England, Scotland and Ireland, and replaced by his daughter Mary II and her husband, William III of Orange. It was both the last successful invasion of England and that of an internal coup. (Below) The death of King James II, September 16, 1701.

Otes Manor House in High Laver, Essex, where Locke spent the last 14 years of his life. He died October 28, 1704, two years following the passing of James II. Locke's relative, Phillip, was 34 at the time. Below is Resurrection House where Phillip & Mary Lock married.

CHAPTER 4:
JAMES SCOTT

Introduction

James Scott, 1st Duke of Monmouth and 1st Duke of Buccleuch, was an English nobleman who was born in the Netherlands. He was born in Rotterdam, Netherlands, as James Crofts or James Fitzroy, and was the eldest illegitimate son of Charles II of England, Scotland, and Ireland and his mistress Lucy Walter.

Before leading the Anglo-Dutch brigade fighting in the Franco-Dutch War, James Scott participated in the Second Anglo-Dutch War and commanded English forces in the Third Anglo-Dutch War. In 1683, he led the disastrous Rye House Plot to assassinate his father, Charles II, and in 1685, he led the unsuccessful Monmouth Rebellion to dethrone his uncle King James II and VII. (Clearly, James Scott was not a family man!) James Scott attempted to profit on his Protestantism and position as the son of Charles II, in opposition to James, who was a Roman Catholic, after one of his officers declared James Scott the lawful monarch in the town of Taunton in Somerset.

Parentage & Early Life

Lucy Walter, who was at The Hague for a short time at this time, charmed Charles, Prince of Wales during the summer of 1648. He was barely eighteen years old at the time, and she is frequently referred to as his first mistress, but they may have had a tryst as early as 1646.

During the Second English Civil War, Charles moved to The Hague, where his sister Mary and brother-in-law William II, Prince of Orange, were more supportive of his father Charles I's cause than his French cousins.

James was born on April 9, 1649, in Rotterdam, Netherlands, and spent his early years in Schiedam. According to some sources, Charles II did not arrive in The Hague until the middle of September 1648, seven months before James Scott was born, but he saw Lucy in July. Lucy was the mistress of Colonel Robert Sidney, the Earl of

Leicester's younger son, in the summer of 1648, according to some whispers. When the boy reached adulthood, supporters of the Duke of York publicized the claim that he resembled Sidney. These voices may have been bolstered by the Duke of York, King Charles II's brother, who was fearful of any of the recognized 14 royal bastards' claims to the throne, given that Charles had no legitimate living offspring. In 2012, a DNA test revealed that the 10th Duke of Buccleuch, a patrilineal descendant of James Scott, shared the same Y chromosome as a distant Stuart cousin. This proves that Charles II was definitely the father of James Scott.

Mary Crofts, James Scott's younger sister or half-sister, may have had Lord Taaffe as a father. Mary eventually married an Irishman, William Sarsfield, and became the Jacobite general Patrick Sarsfield's sister-in-law.

James Scott was unable to inherit to the English or Scottish thrones as an illegitimate son unless he could confirm reports that his parents had secretly married. James Scott eventually claimed that his parents were married and that he had proof of their union, but he never showed it. Charles II later declared to his Council in writing that he had never married anybody other than Catherine of Braganza, the queen.

Young James was kidnapped by one of the King's troops in March 1658, brought to Paris, and placed in the care of a man named John Crofts, whom he briefly adopted as his surname.

Officer & Commander

James was named Duke of Monmouth on February 14, 1663, at the age of 13 and shortly after being transported to England, with the subsidiary titles of Earl of Doncaster and Baron Scott of Tynedale, all three in the Peerage of England, and he was awarded a Knight of the Garter on March 28, 1663.

He married Anne Scott, 4th Countess of Buccleuch, on April 20, 1663, just a few days after his 14th birthday. When James married, he took his wife's surname, which was typical at the time. The pair was named Duke and Duchess of Buccleuch, Earl and Countess of Dalkeith, and Lord and Lady Scott of Whitchester and Eskdale in the Peerage of Scotland the day following their wedding. The formal successor presumptive to the throne, the King's brother James, Duke of York, had openly converted to Roman Catholicism, but James Scott was popular, notably for his Protestantism.

James Scott served in the English fleet in the Second Anglo-Dutch War under his uncle, the Duke of York, when he was 16 years old. He returned to England in June 1666 to take command of a cavalry troop. He was promoted to colonel of the His Majesty's Own Troop of Horse Guards on September 16, 1668. In April 1670, he purchased Moor Park in Hertfordshire. When the Third Anglo-Dutch War broke out in 1672, a brigade of 6,000 English and Scottish troops, led by James Scott, was ordered to join the French army in exchange for money paid to King Charles. In April 1673, he was appointed Lord Lieutenant of the East Riding of Yorkshire and Governor of Kingston-upon-Hull. James Scott earned a reputation as one of Britain's best troops during the 1673 battle, particularly during the Siege of Maastricht in June. He was supposed to take over as commander of England's Zealand Expedition from Marshal Schomberg, but that never happened.

James Scott was appointed Chancellor of Cambridge University and Master of the Horse in 1674, and King Charles II commanded that all military orders be brought to James Scott for inspection first, giving him effective command of the soldiers. The mobilization of troops and the suppression of disturbances were among his tasks. He was also appointed Lord Lieutenant of Staffordshire in March 1677.

Claim to the Crown

James Scott was the leader of the Anglo-Dutch brigade, now fighting for the United Provinces against the French, in 1678, and he distinguished himself at the Battle of Saint-Denis in August of that year during the Franco-Dutch War, enhancing his reputation even further. He commanded the little army raised to put down the Scottish Covenanter uprising the following year, and although being badly outnumbered, he decisively beat the Covenanter rebels at the Battle of Bothwell Bridge on June 22, 1679, though the rebels had inadequate equipment.

As his popularity with the masses increased, James Scott was necessitated to go into exile in September 1679 in the Dutch United Provinces of the Netherlands. But by now, his education, upbringing, military background, and reputation, not to mention his sheer ego, incubated the idea that he should rule Great Britain. Compounded with his father's political leanings and religious overtones to Catholicism, the need to replace Charles II and his heir, James, Duke of York, was obvious. And in four years, James Scott would have his opportunity to do exactly that.

CHAPTER 5:
PHILLIP LOCKE

Preamble

Before we address Phillip Locke, it's important to first place James Scott within the historical relationship of Phillip and his relative, John Locke. Given his birth circumstance as the first (illegitimate) son of Charles II, James Scott was the holder of numerous titles and designations. Besides the initial and most popular-known as 1st Duke of Monmouth, he was also bestowed throughout the years with the following subsidiary titles:

- Earl of Doncaster
- Baron Scott of Tynedale
- Knight of the Garter
- Duke of Buccleuch
- Earl of Dalkeith
- Lord of Whitchester and Eskdale
- Colonel of the His Majesty's Own Troop of Horse Guards
- Lord Lieutenant of the East Riding of Yorkshire
- Governor of Kingston-upon-Hull
- Chancellor of Cambridge University
- Master of the Horse
- Lord Lieutenant of Staffordshire
- Judge, Somerset County, England

Somerset is a county in southwest England. It borders Gloucestershire and Bristol to the north, Wiltshire to the east, Dorset to the southeast, and Devon to the southwest. It is bounded to the north and to the west by the Severn Estuary and the Bristol Channel. Its coastline faces southeastern Wales. Its historic border with Gloucestershire is the River Avon. Somerset is also the location of John Locke's birth, having been born August 1632 in a small, thatched cottage in Wrington, Somerset, roughly 12 miles southwest of Bristol. At the time of his birth, Locke's father, also named John, was an attorney serving as clerk to the Justices of the Peace in Chew Magna, located seven miles due east of Wrington. Soon after John's birth, the family moved to the town of Pensford, about seven miles south of Bristol. The bottom line is that the Locke family and their immediate relatives had roots in the greater Somerset region.

Somerset is a rural county of rolling hills. The county played a significant part in Alfred the Great's rise to power, (later) the English Civil War, and of course, the Monmouth Rebellion, which was James Scott's attempt to overthrow his uncle, James II. In 1685, the Monmouth Rebellion was played out in Somerset, as well as the neighboring district of Dorset.

Somerset is also the home of "HM Prison Shepton Mallet", England's oldest prison, which was still in use prior to its closure in 2013. It was here that James Scott serviced as Judge of Somerset County. HMP Shepton Mallet, sometimes known as 'Cornhill', is a former facility of imprisonment located in Shepton Mallet, Somerset. The prison was established as a 'house of correction' back in 1625. The institution was to comply with the 1610 Bridewell Act of King James I, who required that every county in England have such a house. At the time all prisoners, men, women, and children, were held together in reportedly dreadful conditions. The jailer was not compensated; instead, he earned money by charging fees to his inmates, for example, for furnishing them with alcohol. The house of correction was noted as being in bad repair by the end of the First English Civil War in 1646. At least 12 local men were detained at the Shepton Mallet at the Bloody Assizes following the Monmouth Rebellion before being hanged, drawn, and quartered at the Market Cross.

While serving as a Judge in Somerset County, James Scott's barbarity towards those accused is well documented. He was directly involved in ordering the hanging of at least 350 people, the sale of another 850 as slaves, and the fining, imprisoning, and torturing of 408 others. However, there was also a "humane" side to James Scott. For as another area of his responsibilities, he personally arranged the immigration of English "freemen" or "better sort of people" to aid the British Crown in populating the newly formed colonies in North America. England had initially failed attempts to build permanent colonies in the North began colonization operations in the 17th century. In 1607, Jamestown, Virginia became the first permanent British settlement. At the time, the region was home to some 30,000 Algonquian people. More colonies were formed in North America, Central America, South America, and the Caribbean over the next several centuries. Despite the fact that most British colonies in the Americas eventually obtained independence, certain colonies have chosen to remain British Overseas Territories.

In 1670, the year of Phillip Locke's birth, by royal license, Charles II established the Hudson's Bay Company, giving it a monopoly on the fur trade in Rupert's Land. The French attacked the Company's forts and trading sites on a regular basis. King James II and his governor, Edmund Andros, strove to assert the crown's power over colonial matters after replacing his brother Charles in 1685. In the Glorious Revolution, King James was deposed by the new joint monarchy of William and Mary, but many of James's colonial policies, such as the mercantilist Navigation Acts and the Board of Trade, were immediately revived by William and Mary. The Province of Massachusetts Bay was formed by combining the Massachusetts Bay Colony, Plymouth Colony, and the Province of Maine, and New York and the Massachusetts Bay Colony were restructured as royal colonies with a governor nominated by the king. Maryland, which had seen a revolt against the Calvert family, became a royal colony as well, though the Calverts kept much of their land and money.

Sometime before the Rye House Plot was even planned, John Locke approached James Scott and requested a favor. One of John's young relatives, by the name of Phillip, had expressed interest in traveling to the Americas. Given the fact that John Locke was a shareholder and beneficiary of the slave-trading Royal Africa Company, not to mention Locke's positions as Secretary of the Board of Trade and Plantations and Secretary to the Lords Proprietors of Carolina, discussions of the British Colonies and the opportunities they presented most certainly circulated during Locke family gatherings. As with many males his age, young Phillip was intrigued with the romanticism of traveling to the New World for his country, to seek his own destiny and fortune.

At the time, Charles II encouraged the development of the Colonies as new sources of wealth and power, granting charters to groups of businessmen who offered to help colonists settle in the "New World". Charles also had the advantage of his own illegitimate son, James Scott, to seek out the right sort of men to immigrate to the Colonies. And given Phillip's specialized talents in areas such as craftsman or surveyor, James Scott found young Phillip to be the perfect candidate, personally arranging the necessary paperwork during the first quarter of 1683. Besides, it would seem that James Scott owed John Locke a favor, given, at the very least, the arrangements Locke had made for the accommodations of Scott's group of conspirators. However, Phillip's journey to America was put on hold when a plan to assassinate King Charles II and his brother, the Duke of York, went terribly wrong.

PART TWO: THE PLOT

Walcot & other Conspirators ready to charge ÿ K. Guards

CHAPTER 6:
THE RYE
HOUSE PLOT

Preamble

In recent years it has become widely accepted that John Locke was involved, perhaps deeply involved, in a conspiracy to assassinate King Charles II and his brother, James, Duke of Scott, in 1683. This scheme is historically referred to as "The Rye House Plot". There are claims Locke was not only closely involved with many of the plotters, but that he actually attended some of their meetings. It is also now maintained that Locke's letters of reference contain coded citations to their activities, and that he hastily left London immediately after realizing he had been betrayed.

Thus far, the evidence against Locke, as well as his intellectual reasoning to involve himself in such a scheme to liquidate a king, has been substantial. The evidence goes beyond simply his writings of political and religious viewpoints. Actions speak louder than words. And his association with other conspirators as well as his documented activities prior to and following the event speak volumes in regard to Locke's direct involvement. The involvement, and that of James Scott,

Historians disagree on the extent to which the conspiracy's specifics were ironed out. Whatever the status of the assassination plot, some opposition leaders in England were considering mounting an insurrection against the queen. In a series of state trials, the government used harsh tactics, including coercive measures and broad searches for weapons. The Plot foreshadowed and maybe accelerated the 1685 rebellions, the Monmouth Rebellion and Argyll's Rising.

Introduction

The Rye House Plot of 1683 was a plan to assassinate King Charles II of England and his brother, James, Duke of York, who was heir to the throne. The royal party traveled from Westminster, a

74

district in central London, to the market town of Newmarket, located some 60 miles northeast of Westminster. The purpose of the outing was to see the horse races with an expected return trip on April 1. Rye House, a fortified mediaeval mansion located between Westminster and Newmarket, was the planned location of the attack.

As fate would have it, a major fire had occurred in Newmarket on March 22, which destroyed half the town. The fire caused the obvious cancellation of the races, compelling the King and the Duke to return to London early. As a result, the planned assassination never took place.

The following June, an informant provided details of the Plot to a monarchy diplomat who then uncovered the conspiracy and its participants. Following numerous arrests and trials, King Charles II subsequently had twelve of the conspirators executed, while eleven were imprisoned, and ten were either exiled or fled before an arrest could be made. John Locke, his relative Phillip, and James Scott were among the latter.

Background

Following Charles II's restoration of the monarchy in 1660, several members of Parliament, former republicans, and portions of the Protestant populace of England expressed worry that the King's relationship with France under Louis XIV and other Catholic monarchs of Europe was too tight. Anti-Catholic prejudice, which connected Roman Catholicism with absolute monarchy, was widespread, and the succession to the English throne drew special attention. While Charles and his brother, James, Duke of York, were nominally Anglicans, they were known to have Catholic sympathies. When James was revealed to have converted to Roman Catholicism in 1673, these concerns were confirmed.

The Exclusion Bill was tabled in the House of Commons in 1681, sparked by the opposition-invented Popish Plot, which would have prevented James from succeeding to the throne after Charles' death. The Oxford Parliament was dissolved after Charles outmaneuvered his opponents. As a result, his opponents had no legal way to stop James from succeeding, and suspicions of plans and conspiracies abounded. Lord Melville, Lord Leven, and Lord Ashley, the leaders of the opposition to Charles's authority, escaped to Holland, where Ashley died soon after. Many prominent members of Parliament and noblemen from the "country party" became known as Whigs, a moniker that persisted. One of them was undoubtedly John Locke.

It must be remembered that in 1666, Locke met Lord Ashley who had come to Oxford seeking treatment for a liver infection. Ashley was so impressed with Locke that he persuaded him to become part of his personal entourage. As a founder of the Whig movement, Lord Ashley exerted great influence on Locke's political philosophies. Locke then became highly involved in politics when Ashley became Lord Chancellor in 1672. Ashley was also made 1st Earl of Shaftesbury in 1673.

The so-called Popish Plot, 'revealed' by Titus Oates in the summer of 1678, in which Catholics were alleged to be plotting to assassinate Charles II and his brother, or to kill Charles exclusively and replace him with the Catholic James, was still fresh in the popular memory. Following dramatic depositions and the sensational 'murder' of examining magistrate Edmund Berry Godfrey, Oates' story crumbled during subsequent court hearings in 1679 and 1680; by 1681, his claims were widely disbelieved, and protestant fears of the impending arrival of a 'popish' monarch had been allayed.

The Whig 'party,' which had mostly grown around this cause, began to disintegrate after its failure that year in the Oxford parliament to ensure James' exclusion from the succession to the throne. For the next two years, Charles II and the anti-exclusionist Tories utilized the law to punish their opponents and initiated quo warranto proceedings to seize control of town and county corporations, and via them, any future House of Commons. The acquisition of the City of London's charter was supposed to be the campaign's pinnacle. Faced with this pressure and without a House of Commons to utilize as a platform for their battle, the Whig leadership had resorted to plotting or (at the very least) talking about other forms of resistance.

Ashley was clearly a driving force behind these plans. Although much of the evidence for his role in the plot was only revealed after he was dead and thus unable to defend himself, it is clear that Ashley's greatest fear in his final days was that the Tories would seize control of the government of London, where the former republican Slingsby Bethel and the nonconformist Henry Cornish had used their joint shrievalty of 1680–81 to advance the cause of the nonconformists.

The Conservatives appeared to be on the verge of capturing London's juries, opening the path for Ashley's trial and execution. He eventually escaped to the Low Countries, where he died in January 1683, frustrated with his fellow Whigs, suffering from worsening ill health, and facing imprisonment. As a result, the Whigs' leadership was taken over by the so-called council of six (James Scott, Russell, Essex, Howard of Escrick, Algernon Sidney, and John Hampden). Secret meetings were rumored to be taking place soon after.

Rye House & the Plan

Rye House, located north-east of Hoddesdon, Hertfordshire, was a fortified mediaeval mansion surrounded by a moat. Located just 18 miles northeast of Westchester/London, and on a direct route to Newmarket, the house was leased by a republican and Civil War veteran, Richard Rumbold. One of the Plot's conspirators. The ownership of Rye House had been fairly stable over four centuries. But the structure gradually ran down, and the buildings became diminished. To date, the gatehouse is the only surviving part of the structure.

The aim was to hide a force of assassins in the grounds of Rye House and ambush the King and Duke as they went by on their way back to London from the Newmarket horse races. Newmarket is a market town located 65 miles northeast of London in the English county of Suffolk. It is widely regarded as the origin of thoroughbred horse racing and the current global center of the sport. It is still the country's largest racehorse training and breeding facility, as well as the home of most important British horseracing organizations and a key global hub for horse health. Thereafter the reign of James I, who erected a palace there, the town has had close royal ties, and it has served as a base for Charles I, Charles II, and most monarchs since. Even Queen Elizabeth II comes to view her horses in training on a regular basis.

The idea was to ambush the king's coach on its way back from the races in Newmarket. The killers would use blunderbusses to shoot the postillion and carriage horses and block the passage with a cart in a narrow road. Some assassins would then fire directly into the coach, with Rumbold assigned to murder the king, while others would attack the monarch's guards.

It was an extremely practical idea, reminiscent of prior conspiracies against Oliver Cromwell in the 1650s or Charles II in the 1660s and later 1670s. It also foreshadowed the assassination plot against William III in 1696. The assassinations of James Sharp, archbishop of St Andrews, in 1679, and Thomas Thynne, immediately after he had dropped off his passenger, James Scott, were both carried out by ambushing or overtaking the victims as they traveled in coaches. The plotters of spring 1683, on the other hand, were still in a condition of uncertainty when their chance came and went.

The "Rye House plotters," an extremist Whig group named after this scheme, are said to have chosen the plan out of a variety of options because it had tactical benefits and could be carried out with a small team working with firearms from good cover.

King Charles and the Duke of York were expected to make the journey back to London on April 1, 1683. But a major fire on March 22 in Newmarket literally destroyed half of the town, thereby cancelling the races. So, the King and the Duke returned to London early. As a result of the change in plans, the scheduled assassination never took place.

A larger insurgency was also planned, but the planning was even more hazy in this case. It could have been part of the assassination plot, or it could have been completely unrelated to it. What is evident is that the major Whigs, including, until his death, Ashley, were to have led this section of the plot, and that their discourse (loosened by drink) had been of taking the king rather than killing him. This is not unexpected, given that they were gentlemen and aristocrats, unlike the murder plotters. James Scott, the rash Russell, Sir Thomas Armstrong, Lord Grey, and occasionally others like Ferguson and Howard of Escrick are believed to have gathered in the summer of 1682 and early 1683 to discuss the right of resistance and prospective uprisings in London, Cheshire, and the west country.

James Scott and a few others were said to have gone out one dark night to inspect the king's soldiers' alertness around Whitehall. To the dismay of the increasingly frantic Ashley, who claimed that 1000 men from Wapping, his so-called 'brisk lads,' would join an insurgency and talked of seizing the Tower of London, these meetings mostly remained an unrealistic and insignificant talking shop. He may have also encouraged the murder plot's more hot-headed parts in his crazier moments. After Ashley had departed, the leadership transferred to the council of six, although the members' priorities were drastically different. While James Scott was cautious in order to establish and retain his position as a future heir to the throne, Sidney was a firm believer in the republican cause.

Other Conspirators

The sheer number of conspirators during this time were numerous! On what was becoming the "Whig" side of the dissenting division of British politics, the recourse to follow through with an armed resistance against Charles II was widely deliberated from the early 1680s. Exactly how an armed confrontation would take place was uncertain, through there were discussions of controlling British cities other than London, including Bristol and even towns in Scotland. The subsequent planning and scheduling of the Plot was largely one sided and, to this date, scholars are still researching who was closely involved in the formation and preparation of violent, revolutionary actions.

The Robert West Conspiracy

The Rye House assassination plot centered on a group that organized in 1682–1683 by a gentleman by the name of Robert West. West was of the Middle Temple, one of the four Inns of Court exclusively entitled to call their members to the English Bar as barristers, was Green Ribbon Club member. This Club was one of the earliest of associations that met from time to time in London coffeehouses and taverns for political purposes. The green ribbon was the badge of the "Levellers" of the English Civil Wars, a political movement committed to extended suffrage, popular sovereignty, religious tolerance, and equality before the law. Many of the green ribbon recipients, including West, had fought in the Civil Wars and stood as an explicit reminder of the radical beginnings of the club's loyalties.

Robert West had partaken in one of the indictments that wound up the Popish Plot allegations, that of the false witness Stephen College, an English joiner, activist Protestant, and supporter of the perjury underlying the fabricated Popish Plot. He was tried and executed for high treason, on somewhat dubious evidence, in 1681.

Through that association, West made contact with Aaron Smith and William Hone, both to be plotters though aside from the main group.

In the meantime, and as verified in documented evidence, John Locke personally arranged accommodations for Robert West in the English city of Oxford. Locke also had numerous associations in the group of revolutionary activists, including Christopher Battiscombe, Israel Hayes, and John Ayloffe. Ayloffe was an English lawyer and political activist. In the UK, he was known as one of the most unswervingly committed radicals against the monarchy.

Throughout his career, John Ayloffe was a hardline opponent of the Stuart monarchy of which Charles II was the head of given his title of king. At the time, Ayloffe was generating a steady stream of propaganda against the monarchy. His writings were characterized by his bitterly anti-Catholic tones. Charles II was, himself, being constantly being compared to tyrants seeking to destroy English liberties by Ayloffe. In addition to his publications, John Ayloffe worked as an intelligence agent for William of Orange and was a loyal ally of Lord Ashley during the Exclusion Crisis of 1679-1680.

Because of his close political alliance with, and support of Ayloffe, John Locke would quickly become susceptible to accusations by the monarchy. As documented in various writings and correspondences, Locke was under suspicion as an accomplice even before the Rye House Plot has been exposed.

Uprising Strategies

Many of the West group's discussions were aligned with the ideas of Algernon Sidney, in particular, and the more aristocratic country party members who made up the so-called Monmouth cabal, with members like Richard Nelthorpe favoring a rebellion over a murder. Among September 1682, there were discussions of an uprising in the group surrounding James Scott, which shared participants with the group around Robert West. The "cabal" was renamed the "council of six" after Tory victories in the battle for control of the City of London in the summer of 1682. The idea to use Archibald Campbell, 9th Earl of Argyll, in a military insurrection in Scotland was a crucial part. Smith was dispatched in January 1683 to contact supporters in Scotland for the "six," with the goal of summoning them to London. He appears to have botched the assignment due to his transgressions.

In actuality, West's interactions with the Monmouth cabal, as well as his awareness of their plans, were mostly indirect. Ashley's self-imposed exile to the Netherlands in November 1682 was accompanied by Thomas Walcot and Robert Ferguson. They both went to London and became involved with West, who had learned about Ashley's own plan for a mass revolt through Walcott. Walcott went on to explain that he would lead the attack on the royal guards, but he was one of the plotters who said that assassination was out of the question.

During the spring of 1683, there were more discussions between the Monmouth cabal and West's group regarding producing a manifesto, particularly through Sir Thomas Armstrong, with differences about whether revolutionary methods should culminate in a republican or monarchical constitution. Both West and Walcott discussed the potential for raising a force of several thousand soldiers around London with a bigger group in May of 1683.

The suspected murder plot appears to be the most severe aspect of the operation. While this encompassed the lower-ranking conspirators, it is still debatable how united they were in their beliefs. Some had a long history of conspiracy behind them, and most had held onto the idea of the "good old cause" since at least the 1650s, such as the old Cromwellian soldiers Rumbold and Rumsey, who had also fought in Portugal; some had a long history of conspiracy behind them, and most had held onto the idea of the "good old cause" since at least the 1650s. They were terrified of Stuart's "slavery," and the military men alone were very than capable of committing acts of violence to resist it. The most likely point of contact with Ashley was West, although Armstrong and Lord Grey of Warke supplied other connections. They were also aware of Ashley's covert meetings with Archibald Campbell, ninth Earl of Argyll, in the summer of 1682, at which a Scottish uprising was discussed.

Following that, a succession of meetings took conducted in taverns and other locations, with 'cant language' used to conceal the plotters' goals. Some plotters felt that assassinating Charles II and replacing him with his protestant successor, James Scott, would prompt the latter to seek vengeance on his father's killers, while others deemed assassination to be dishonorable in and of itself. Some conspirators, on the other hand, favored not only the assassination of Edmund Ludlow, but also his recall to lead the inevitable uprising that would follow. There was also debate over whether the king and Duke of York should be the only targets, as well as whether the weapons used should be consecrated. The Rye House, a house held by former soldier and now maltster Richard Rumbold, was eventually chosen for the assassination of the king and his brother amid considerable drinking (another feature of plotters of the day).

The Plotters

The aristocratic personalities who were drawn into the Rye House scheme included the following:

- Whig leader Lord Ashley, 1st Earl of Shaftesbury
- James Scott, Duke of Monmouth
- John Locke, English British philosopher & Oxford academic
- William Russell aka Lord Russell
- Arthur Capel, first Earl of Essex
- William Howard, third Baron Howard of Escrick
- Algernon Sidney
- Sir Thomas Armstrong, Lord Grey of Warke
- Thomas Grey, second earl of Stamford
- John Hampden, grandson of the notable parliamentary politician

On a lower level of British society were other, perhaps more dangerous, plotters:

- Richard Rumbold, as described earlier
- John Rumsey
- Thomas Walcott, a former lieutenant to the regicide Edmund Ludlow
- Richard Goodenough, a former under-sheriff in London
- Robert West, as described earlier
- Robert Ferguson, Scottish-born professional conspirator, and clergyman

Russell and Sidney's acts were later dubbed *"dissolving the government with a touch of a trigger"* by Roger North, one of the prosecution's lawyers. The strategy was broken into two parts as it emerged through the several interrogations of the accused participants beginning in June 1683. They were (1) the assassination plot and (2) the larger insurgency. The connection between these two sections has always been a mystery, and it has even been disputed at times. King Charles II did not die, and there was no uprising in 1683, as with every historical non-event.

As a result, some historians have struggled to determine the scale and complexity of both projects and have questioned many of the specifics, including who was involved. Some historians have questioned the plot's very existence, despite the overwhelming evidence. Others have claimed that it was provoked or even manufactured by a fearful administration out to eliminate its Whig opponents.

Whatever the reality is, it is evident that the informants engaged were eager to save their own skin in treason trials where guilt was assumed in most cases. It was easy enough to give up others, no matter the relation and no matter the truth behind their confessions. Given the undeniable exaggerations in the extant information, there is little that can be done today to disentangle the situation, but its background is evident enough.

Scottish & American Connections

Colonial plans in America confuse the interpretation of true Whig aims at this period. East Jersey was important to Robert West. Ashley was quite active in the Carolina Province. As Smith had predicted, some Whig contacts from Scotland came in London in April 1683, meeting Essex and Russell of the Monmouth cabal. They were either under the misconception that the situation involved Carolina, or they used it as a pretext to justify their attendance. Sir George Campbell of Cessnock, John Cochrane, and William Carstares were among them.

In August 1682, the Earl of Argyll departed London for the Netherlands, although he maintained contact with Whig leaders through couriers and ciphered correspondence. In June 1683, two of them, William Spence and Abraham Holmes, were captured and subsequently brought to trial.

CHAPTER 7:
INFORMERS
& ARRESTS

On June 12, 1683, Josiah Keeling, a London oil merchant and nonconformist, and a minor intrigue finally betrayed the plot to the government, purportedly moved by guilt or plain dread of the repercussions, and the arrests began. Over the course of the next month or two, a number of those arrested either turned king's evidence or sought a pardon and began incriminating as many of their peers as possible. Even if some of the evidence of the Rye House conspiracy, as well as the actions of its plotters, is questioned, there is little doubt that planning was, in many ways, the only option left to the Whigs' problems in 1683.

Sir Leoline Jenkins learned of the plot from Keeling. Keeling had contacted a courtier, who introduced him to George Legge, 1st Baron Dartmouth, and Dartmouth had introduced him to Jenkins, Secretary of State. Keeling's testimony was used in the trials of Walcott, Hone, Sidney, and Charles Bateman, and he was granted a pardon as a result of it. It also kicked off a lengthy process of incriminated individuals confessing in the hopes of receiving mercy. Keeling was able to obtain additional direct proof of conspiracy through his brother, and Jenkins brought in Rumsey and West on June 23, who told him what they knew; West had offered information via Laurence Hyde, 1st Earl of Rochester, on the 22nd. West recounted the Rye House scheme and his role in procuring weaponry for America over the course of several days. He didn't do much to accuse the James Scott gang, but his testimony was used against Walcott and Sidney afterwards. In December 1684, West was granted a pardon.

Following Keeling's exposure of the conspiracy, several of the suspected conspirators were arrested. Rumsey, West, and Thomas Sheppard, a trader, then presented contradicting information against their colleagues. Sheppard, for example, corroborated Russell and Sidney's involvement in the conspiracy but may have hidden the involvement of other persons.

Some of the testimony was personally inspected by Charles II, who refused to allow the informers to elaborate on their evidence as Titus Oates had done. Sir John Reresby stated the plot was made up of "those who had been disappointed of preferments at Court, and of protestant dissenters"; nonconformists were persecuted as a result. Rumbold, Walcott, and others were ordered to be arrested on June 23. Sidney and Russell were transported to the Tower on June 26th. James Scott, Lord Grey, Armstrong, and Ferguson were each promised £500 as a reward. Grey was apprehended and then escaped, and James Scott had fled the area.

Hampden and Howard of Escrick were apprehended on July 8, and the Earl of Essex was imprisoned in the Tower. Howard, who had a history of surviving conspiracies, gladly accepted a pardon in exchange for telling on his fellow conspirators, and trials were held quickly. During Russell's trial, news of Essex's suicide arrived having slit his own throat in his cell, or some said, had been murdered at the behest of the government. Despite this, Russell was found guilty based on Sheppard and Howard's testimony. Attempts to get a pardon for him were unsuccessful, and he was sentenced to death on July 13th.

In November, the egotistical Sidney was brought to trial. Due to a lack of evidence, Judge George Jeffreys used his own manuscripts on the rights of resistance to trap Sidney, and he was sentenced to death and executed on December 7, 1683. Meanwhile, James Scott had surrendered on the 24th of November after receiving a pardon. Scott disputed the assassination plot while George Savile, first marquess of Halifax, attempted to mediate a reconciliation between the king and his son. However, he signed a document confessing to conspiracy to rebellion on the condition that it not be used as evidence. His demands eventually wore down the king's tolerance and he was exiled. As a result, he was unavailable for Hampden's trial where he was found guilty of a misdemeanor. Following the investigations, arrests, and trials, the following sentences and actions for those accused and/or implicated are as follows:

Executed

- SIR THOMAS ARMSTRONG: Member of Parliament for Stafford; hanged, drawn & quartered
- JOHN AYLOFFE: Hanged, drawn & quartered

- HENRY CORNISH: Sheriff of London; hanged, drawn & quartered
- ELIZABETH GAUNT: Burnt at the stake
- JAMES HOLLOWAY: Hanged, drawn & quartered
- BAILLIE OF JERVISWOOD: Hanged
- RICHARD NELTHORPE: Hanged
- RICHARD RUMBOLD: Hanged, drawn & quartered
- LORD WILLIAM RUSSELL: Member of Parliament for Bedfordshire; beheaded
- ALGERNON SIDNEY: Former Lord Warden; beheaded
- THOMAS WALCOTT: Hanged, drawn & quartered
- JOHN ROUSE: Hanged, drawn & quartered

For those who may be interested, persons convicted of high treason in England in prior centuries were sentenced to be hanged, drawn, and quartered. However, similar ceremonies were documented during King Henry III's reign between 1216 and 1272.

The guilty party was tied to a hurdle, or wooden panel, and brought to the execution site by horse. He was then hanged nearly to death, emasculated, disemboweled, beheaded, and quartered, which means chopped into four pieces. The remains were then frequently placed in prominent locations across the country, as a warning of traitors' fate. Women convicted of high treason were instead burnt at the stake for grounds of public decorum.

The severity of the penalty was determined by the gravity of the offence. High treason was regarded as a heinous offense that deserved the harshest punishment as an attack on the English monarchy's power. Many men judged guilty of high treason were sentenced to the law's ultimate consequence over a period of several hundred years, despite the fact that other convicted had their sentences mitigated and experienced a less shameful death. Many English Catholic priests were executed during the Elizabethan period, as were some regicides implicated in the 1649 execution of Charles I, King Charles II's father.

Although the Act of Parliament defining high treason is still on the books in the United Kingdom, the sentence of hanging, drawing, and quartering was changed to drawing, hanging until dead, and posthumous beheading and quartering during a long period of 19th-century legal reform before being abolished in England in 1870.

Sentenced to Death, but Later Pardoned

- CHARLES GERARD: 1st Earl of Macclesfield
- CHARLES GERARD: Viscount Brandon

Imprisoned

- SIR SAMUEL BARNARDISTON: 1st Baronet, also fined £6,000
- HENRY BOOTH: 1st Earl of Warrington
- PAUL FOLEY: Member of Parliament for Hereford
- THOMAS GREY: 2nd Earl of Stamford
- JOHN HAMPDEN: Member of Parliament for Wendover, also fined £40,000
- WILLIAM HOWARD: 3rd Baron Howard of Escrick. At Lord William Russell's trial, he was arrested and turned informer. He described meetings at John Hampden's and Russell's homes, which were largely responsible for Russell's conviction. Sidney was equally devastated by his testimony.
- MATTHEW MEAD
- AARON SMITH
- SIR JOHN TRENCHARD: Member of Parliament for Taunton
- SIR JOHN WILDMAN

Exiled / Fled

- SIR JOHN COCHRANE: Fled to Holland
- ROBERT FERGUSON: Fled to the Netherlands
- FORD GREY: 3rd Baron Grey of Werke, escaped from the Tower of London
- PATRICK HUME: 1st Earl of Marchmont, fled to the Netherlands
- JAMES SCOTT: Exiled; Fled to the Netherlands
- JOHN LOCKE: Fled to the Netherlands
- PHILLIP LOCKE: Fled to North Ireland
- JOHN LOVELACE: 3rd Baron Lovelace, fled to Holland

- DAVID MELVILLE: 3rd Earl of Leven, fled to the Netherlands
- GEORGE MELVILLE: 1st Earl of Melville, fled to the Netherlands
- EDWARD NORTON: Fled to Holland
- NATHANIEL WADE: Fled to Holland

Committed suicide

- ARTHUR CAPELL: 1st Earl of Essex, cut his own throat in the Tower of London

Tortured

- WILLIAM CARSTARES

Implicated

- ARCHIBALD CAMPBELL: 9th Earl of Argyll, beheaded after Argyll's Rising, although on an earlier 1681 treason charge
- JAMES DALRYMPLE: 1st Viscount of Stair
- EDWARD HUNGERFORD: Member of Parliament for Chippenham
- JOHN OWEN
- JAMES BURTON: He averted punishment by implicating Elizabeth Gaunt, a benevolent Baptist matron, and John Fernley, a poor barber in Whitechapel, both of whom were present when the assassination was discussed by his accomplices.
- JOHN RUMSEY: He escaped arrest on accusations of participation by accusing alderman Henry Cornish.

Charles Bateman faced the Rye House charges for the final time in 1685. The conspirators Keeling, who had nothing specific to say, Thomas Lee, and Richard Goodenough testified against him. Bateman was hung, quartered, and drawn.

Sir William Waller moved to Bremen in 1683 after fleeing abroad the previous year. He became a major character in a group of former conspirators who were in political exile when he was there. The English envoy in Paris, Lord Preston, referred to him as "the governor" and wrote, "They style Waller, by way of compliment, a second Cromwell." Waller would travel to England with William of Orange in 1688, but when William's government was constituted, he opted to ignore him.

While some researchers claim there is little evidence to support John Locke's involvement in the Rye House Plot, there was certainly enough assumed guilt at the time to compel Locke to literally flee for his life from England! With a keen understanding of what was taking place with his political colleagues, and under strong growing susception from the monarchy, Locke quickly packed as best he could and made his way to the southeast coast of England where he caught a ship bound for the Netherlands. Given the fact he was unmarried and childless, his hasty plans to abscond the country were uninhibited. In fact, Locke departed so quickly that he could not make financial arrangements or even pack sufficient clothes.

James Scott, 1st Duke of Monmouth, also escaped to the Netherlands at the same time as John Locke, though some say they fled together on the same ship and kept a close correspondence during their time abroad.

Equally concerned was relative Phillip Locke. His relationship with John and association and recent favoritism from James Scott to immigrate to the British Colonies made him an easy target, at least for an investigation by the government. Not wanting to take chances, and given his inevitable travels to America anyway, young Phillip hastily arranged for the consolidation and bundling of his belongings and trekked in the opposite direction of John Locke; fleeing to northwest England where a ship took him across the Irish Sea to Belfast, Ireland, then on to the nearby County of Antrim, one of six counties that form Northern Ireland as situated in the island's northeast section.

PART THREE: AFTERMATH

A True ACCOUNT
AND
DECLARATION
OF
The Horrid Conspiracy
Against the Late
KING,
His Present MAJESTY,
AND THE
GOVERNMENT:
As it was Order'd to be Published by His late Majesty.

The Second EDITION.

In the SAVOY:
Printed by Thomas Newcomb, One of His Majesties
Printers; and are to be sold by Sam. Lowndes over-
against Exeter-Change in the Strand. 1685.

CHAPTER 8:
CHARLES II;
THE FINAL YEARS

As a result, in the final years of Charles' reign, his attitude toward his opponents shifted, and Whigs compared him to the current Louis XIV of France, whose type of administration was dubbed "slavery" at the time. Many of them were prosecuted and their estates taken, with Charles arbitrarily replacing judges and sheriffs and cramming juries to ensure guilt. To eliminate resistance in London, Charles had earlier disenfranchised numerous Whigs in municipal elections in 1682, and the London charter was forfeited in 1683 after the unsuccessful Rye House Plot. In retrospect, Charles' use of the court system as a weapon against dissent contributed to the establishment of the idea of separation of powers between the judiciary and the Crown in Whig ideology.

On the morning of February 2, 1685, Charles had an apoplectic attack. On February 6, he died at the Palace of Whitehall at 11:45 a.m. at the age of 54. Many people, including one of the royal doctors, suspected poison because of his quick illness and death. However, according to more recent medical research, the symptoms of his terminal sickness are identical to those of uremia, a clinical disease caused by kidney failure.

Charles had a laboratory among his numerous interests, where he had been experimenting with mercury before to his illness. Mercuric overdose can result in kidney damage that is irreversible. However, there is no proof that this was the cause of his death. Charles underwent a number of excruciating therapies in the days leading up to his death, including bloodletting, purging, and cupping, in the hopes of regaining consciousness. These medications may have aggravated his uremia by dehydrating him rather than alleviating it.

Charles instructed his brother, James, to watch after his mistresses on his deathbed. *"Go well, Portsmouth, and don't let poor Nelly go hungry."* To his courtiers he stated, *"I apologize, gentlemen, for being such a time a-dying."* He then subsequently expressed regret for the way he had treated his wife. He was admitted into the Catholic Church in the presence of Father John Huddleston on the last evening of his life, though it is unknown to what extent he was completely cognizant or committed, or with whence the notion originated. On February 14, he was laid to rest in Westminster Abbey without fanfare. James II, Charles' brother, succeeded him as king.

Charles' exploits following his defeat at the Battle of Worcester remained important to him for the rest of his life. For many years, he entertained and bored listeners with tales of his escape. Several tales of his exploits were published, especially in the aftermath of the Restoration. Though he was not opposed to his escape being attributed to divine providence, Charles appears to have taken pride in his ability to maintain his disguise as a commoner and walk unnoticed through his domain. Charles, ironic and cynical, delighted in telling anecdotes that revealed the invisibility of any inherent magnificence he possessed.

Charles had no legitimate offspring, but seven mistresses acknowledged a dozen, including five by Barbara Villiers, Lady Castlemaine, for whom the Dukedom of Cleveland was established. Moll Davis, Nell Gwyn, Elizabeth Killigrew, Catherine Pegge, Lucy Walter, and Louise de Kérouaille, Duchess of Portsmouth were among his numerous mistresses. As a result, he was known as "Old Rowley" during his lifetime, after his favorite racehorse, who was also a stallion.

His subjects despised paying taxes to support his mistresses and their children, many of whom were granted dukedoms or earldoms. The current Dukes of Buccleuch, Richmond, Grafton, and St Albans are all male descendants of Charles. Diana, Princess of Wales, was descended from the Dukes of Grafton and Richmond, two of Charles's illegitimate offspring. Prince William, Duke of Cambridge, Diana's son and the second in line to the British throne, is expected to be the first king descended from Charles II.

Tories tended to see Charles' reign as a period of beneficent monarchy, whilst Whigs saw it as a period of horrible despotism. Today, he is considered as more of a lovable rogue—"a prince of many qualities and many vast flaws, debonair, ease of access, neither bloody or cruel," as his contemporary John Evelyn put it. More lewdly, John Wilmot, 2nd Earl of Rochester, wrote about Charles:

"Restless he rolls from whore to whore
A merry monarch, scandalous and poor."

His polarized historiography might be summarized in this way: Books on Charles II have been split into two categories during the past hundred years. Academic historians have focused mostly on his efforts as a statesman, emphasizing his deceit, self-indulgence, bad judgment, and lack of aptitude for commerce or steady and reliable government. Non-academic authors have primarily focused on his social and cultural milieu, highlighting his charm, affability, worldliness, and tolerance, making him one of the most popular English kings in books, plays, and films.

In his day, Charles was a beloved king and a "legendary figure" in British history. Other kings had garnered more admiration, but only Henry VIII had endeared himself to the public imagination to the extent that he had. He was the mischievous but nice playboy monarch, the hero of those who valued urbanity, tolerance, good humor, and the pursuit of pleasure over more serious, sober, or material values.

Until the mid-nineteenth century, the anniversary of the Restoration, which was also Charles' birthday, was known in England as Oak Apple Day, after the Royal Oak in which Charles sheltered during his escape from Oliver Cromwell's army. Oak leaves were once worn as part of traditional celebrations, but this practice has since gone out. In art, literature, and the media, Charles II is frequently depicted. He is commemorated in the cities of Charleston, South Carolina, and South Kingstown, Rhode Island.

Upon the death of Charles II, James II immediately became King of England and Ireland, and later as James VII adding Scotland to his monarchy. He ruled until the "Glorious Revolution" in 1688, when he was ousted. He was England's, Scotland's, and Ireland's last Catholic monarch, and his reign is now recognized mostly for religious tolerance fights. However, it also encompassed the notions of absolutism and divine right of monarchs, and his overthrow confirmed Parliament's primacy over the Crown, putting an end to a century of political and civil strife.

With overwhelming support in all three nations, James inherited the thrones of England, Ireland, and Scotland, mostly based on the notions of divine right or birth. When the English and Scottish Parliaments refused to accept his measures, James attempted to impose them by decree; ultimately, it was a political principle, not a religious one, that led to his ouster.

Two occurrences in June 1688 pushed discontent into a catastrophe. The birth of James's son and successor James Francis Edward on June 10 threatened to establish a Roman Catholic dynasty, excluding his Anglican daughter Mary and her Protestant husband William III of Orange. The prosecution of the Seven Bishops for seditious libel was the second. This was seen as a direct attack on the Church of England, and their acquittal on June 30 effectively ended his political power in England. Anti-Catholic rioting in England and Scotland made it appear that only his abdication would avoid a civil war.

William of Orange was asked to take the English throne by leading members of the English political establishment. James' troops left him after he landed at Brixham on November 5, 1688, and he went into exile in France on December 23. In February 1689, a special Parliament declared that the king had "vacated" the English throne and placed William and Mary as joint monarchs, establishing the notion that power came from Parliament rather than birth. On March 14, 1689, James landed in Ireland in an attempt to reclaim his kingdoms. Despite a parallel uprising in Scotland, the Scottish Convention followed the English one in April, declaring that James had "forfeited" the crown and offered it to William and Mary. Following his loss at the Battle of the Boyne in July 1690, James retreated to France and spent the rest of his life in exile at Saint-Germain, under Louis XIV's protection. Despite his opponents' portrayals of him as an absolutist ruler, historians in the twentieth century commended him for preaching religious tolerance, and more recent scholarship has attempted to establish a medium ground between the two points of view.

CHAPTER 9:
JAMES SCOTT'S
LAST STAND

Following the death of King Charles II in February 1685, James Scott led the Monmouth Rebellion, landing with three ships in Lyme Regis, Dorset, in early June 1685, in an effort to usurp the crown from his uncle, James II and VII. He issued a *"Declaration for the defense and vindication of the protestant religion and of the laws, rights, and privileges of England from the invasion made upon them, and for delivering the Kingdom from the usurpation and tyranny of us by the name of James, Duke of York,"* to which King James II responded by ordering the arrest of the paper's publishers.

At different points along the road, including Axminster, Chard, Ilminster, and Taunton, James Scott declared himself the lawful King. James Scott's patchwork force could not match with the regular army, and was decisively defeated at the Fight of Sedgemoor on July 6, 1685, the last clear-cut pitched battle on open field between two military forces fought on English territory.

Capture

Following the conflict, a reward was announced for the capture of James Scott. On July 8, 1685, he was apprehended near Ringwood, Hampshire, *"in a field of peas"* according to legend. The events leading up to his capture are detailed in Tait's Edinburgh Magazine.

On the 7th, around 5 a.m., some of Lord Lumley's said scouts riding in the road near Holt Lodge in Dorset, four miles west of Ringwood in Hampshire, just at the turn of a cross way, surprised and apprehended two suspected persons, who were later identified as Lord Grey and Hollyday the guide when the Lord Lumley arrived. Lord Lumley then began a thorough inspection of the cottages that were strewn over this lush countryside, and he enlisted the help of individuals who were familiar with the area. Sir William Portman was alerted to the capture and rushed to the scene with as many of his horse and footmen as he could muster. While Lord Lumley was questioning the cottagers, a poor woman named Amy Farrant pointed him to a hedge where she had seen two men go. The outbounds of numerous fenced fields, some overgrown with fern and brakes and others seeded with rye, peas, and oats, revealed this hedge. While horse and foot did their allotted duties, the assembled militia were deployed around these outbounds, at short distances from each other.

When the Duke abandoned his horse at Woodyates Inn, he swapped clothing with a shepherd, who was quickly identified and interrogated by local loyalists. The dogs were then trained to follow the Duke's smell. James Scott threw his gold snuff-box, which was full of gold coins, into a pea-field, where it was later discovered.

The Duke had traveled from Woodyates Inn to Shag's Heath, which featured a cluster of small farms known as the "Island" in the midst. The fugitives were hidden within the Island, according to Amy Farrant. The Duke remained hidden all day, escorted by Busse and Brandenburgher, with soldiers encircling the spot and threatening to set fire to the woods. At 1:00 a.m., Brandenburgher fled him, was later apprehended and interrogated, and is believed to have revealed the Duke's hiding position. The location was in Lord Ashley's manor of Woodlands, at the north-eastern tip of the Island, now known as Monmouth's Close. At around 7:00 a.m., Henry Parkin, a militia soldier and servant of Samuel Rolle, spotted James Scott's brown coat skirt hidden in a ditch covered in fern and brambles behind an ash tree and sought for help. The Duke was apprehended. Bystanders yelled, "Shoot him! shoot him!" but Sir William Portman, who happened to be near the scene, rode up and took him as his prisoner. Monmouth was the name of the town at the time in the throes of hunger and exhaustion, with nothing to eat but a few raw peas in his pocket. He couldn't stand up, and his appearance had changed dramatically. The Duke had not gotten a good night's sleep or eaten a meal in peace since arriving in England, and he was continuously irritated by the anxieties that come with unfortunate ambition, he had *"got no other sustenance than that which the brook and the field provided."*

The Duke was taken to Holt Lodge, a magistrate's residence about a mile away in the parish of Wimborne, who asked the Duke what he would do if he was released, to which he replied, *"That if his horse and arms were only restored to him at the same time, he needed only to ride through the army; and he defied them to take him again."* The Judge ordered that he be sent to London.

Attainder & Execution

Following James Scott's capture, the British Parliament passed an "Act of Attainder", which read as follows:

"Treason. Whereas James Duke of Monmouth has in an hostile Manner Invaded this Kingdom and is now in open Rebellion Laying War against the King contrary to the Duty of his Allegiance, Be it enacted by the Kings most Excellent Majesty by and with the Advice and Consent of the Lords Spiritual and Temporal and Commons in this Parliament assembled and by the Authorities of the same, That the said James Duke of Monmouth Stand and be Convicted and Attainted of High-Treason and that he suffer Paines of Death and Incurr all Forfeitures as a Traitor Convicted and Attainted of High Treason."

The King took the unprecedented step of giving his nephew an audience even though he had no intention of pardoning him, breaking with a long-standing custom that the King would only provide an audience when he meant to show clemency. The prisoner begged for his mercy unsuccessfully, even offering to convert to Catholicism, but to no avail. Disgusted by his depravity, the King told him to "prepare to die", later remarking that James Scott *"did not act as nicely as I expected."* The King received numerous requests for clemency, including one from his sister-in-law, the Dowager Queen Catherine, but he ignored them all.

On July 15, 1685, on Tower Hill, James Scott was decapitated by Jack Ketch. Scott was 36 years old. Bishops Turner of Ely and Ken of Bath and Wells had visited the Duke to prepare him for eternity, but they refused to give him the Eucharist because he refused to admit that his rebellion or his relationship with Lady Wentworth had been wicked. James Scott is believed to have demanded that Ketch finish him in one blow before laying his head on the block, claiming that he has mauled others before. Disturbed, Ketch struck the prisoner many times with his axe, with Scott rising up reproachfully in the process; a gruesome sight that horrified the bystanders, eliciting screams and cries. Some claim that a knife was finally used to separate the head from the quivering body. Some sources indicate it took eight blows, whereas the official Tower of London fact page claims it took five. In the film "Kind Hearts and Coronets", his execution is referred to, with the executioner saying *"The last time a duke was executed in this country, it went horribly wrong. But that was back when the axe was used."*

James Scott was buried in the Tower of London's Church of St Peter ad Vincula. His Dukedom was forfeited, but his subsidiary titles of Earl of Doncaster and Baron Scott of Tindale were restored to his grandson Francis Scott, 2nd Duke of Buccleuch, by King George II on March 23, 1743.

Popular legends

According to folklore, a painting of James Scott was painted after his execution because it was discovered that there was no official portrait of the Duke after his execution, so his body was exhumed, the head stitched back on, and it was seated for its portrait to be painted. However, the National Portrait Gallery in London has at least two formal portraits of James Scott likely dated to before his death, as well as another artwork historically associated with James Scott that depicts a sleeping or dead man, which could have sparked the narrative.

One of the many theories about The Man in the Iron Mask's identity is that he was James Scott: this appears to be based on the improbable logic that James II would not execute his own nephew, so someone else was executed instead, and James II arranged for James Scott to be taken to France and placed in the custody of his cousin Louis XIV of France.

CHAPTER 10:
THE LOCKE'S
ENDURE

John Locke; Exile & Return

Locke fled to the Netherlands in 1683, under suspicion of complicity in the Rye House Plot, as previously mentioned. Locke chose his acquaintances from among the same freethinking members of dissenting Protestant groups as Spinoza's small network of close confidants, according to philosopher and author Rebecca Newberger Goldstein. In Amsterdam, Locke probably certainly encountered men who shared his thoughts and ideas. While Locke's strong empiricist tendencies would have prevented him from reading a grandly metaphysical text, he was open to ideas centered on a rationalist's well-thought-out argument for political and religious tolerance, as well as the importance of church-state separation.

Locke had time in the Netherlands to return to his writing, and he spent much of it working on the "Essay Concerning Human Understanding" and drafting the "Letter on Toleration." After the Glorious Revolution, when James II and VII, kings of England, Scotland, and Ireland, were deposed and replaced by his daughter Mary II and her husband, William III of Orange, Locke did not return to England. In reality, five years after the Rye House Plot, Locke escorted Mary II back to England in 1688. After his return from exile, Locke published the majority of his works, including the aforementioned "Essay Concerning Human Understanding," the "Two Treatises of Government," and "A Letter Concerning Toleration." All three show up at the same time.

Lady Masham, Locke's close friend, invited him to join her at the Mashams' country estate in Essex, "Otes." Despite suffering from asthma attacks and other health concerns during his time there, he became a Whig intellectual hero. During this time, he met with John Dryden and Isaac Newton to discuss many topics.

The English Restoration, the Great Plague of London, the Great Fire of London, and the Glorious Revolution all occurred during Locke's lifetime. Despite the fact that the thrones of England and

Scotland were held in personal union throughout his lifetime, he did not live long enough to witness the Act of Union of 1707. During Locke's day, constitutional monarchy and parliamentary democracy were still in their infancy.

John Locke died on October 28, 1704, at the age of 72. He was buried in the churchyard of High Laver, Essex, east of Harlow, where he had lived in Sir Francis Masham's household since 1691. Locke never married, nor did he have children.

Phillip Lock(e); a Life in America

Sometime in 1687, Phillip Lock boarded a ship that took him from (possibly) Ireland to America. There are no records to indicate any other Lock family members traveling across the Atlantic with Phillip; no mention of a parent or sibling in any of the available data residing in Maryland, nor any early colony for that matter. It is assumed then that Phillip made the journey alone.

If Phillip did indeed carry the L-O-C-K-E surname during his life in England, it's assumed he was compelled to drop the "E" as an attempt to cover his true identity as a relative of John Locke and benefactor of James Scott. Of course, despite the name on any ship manifest, Phillip would have kept on his possession documented evidence of his true identity upon arrival to America in order to position himself among the regional plantation owners, which he did successfully.

After two harrowing months at sea, the ship carrying Phillip Lock landed at the greater coastal area of what would later be the State of New Jersey. From there Phillip traveled through Philadelphia where, just five years earlier, William Penn, an English real estate entrepreneur, founded the city to serve as the capital of the Pennsylvania Colony which was named after him.

From Philadelphia, Phillip Lock made his way to the town of Baltimore where, 26 years earlier, English colonists had begun to settle. It would be another 19 years following Phillip's arrival in Maryland that the colony's General Assembly would create the 'Port of Baltimore' in 1706 for the tobacco trade of which Phillip would someday be a part of. Continuing southward past Baltimore, Phillip eventually settled in St. Mary's County, Maryland, located on the very southern tip of the colony's peninsula landmass, with the Chesapeake Bay to the east and the Potomac River to the south and west. Of course, at this time, there was no formal State of Maryland, and no United States of America. Independence from Britain wouldn't come for another 89 years.

Phillip Lock was most likely some type of specialized craftsman or surveyor as it would appear he positioned himself well to work with the established plantation families in St. Mary's County. And it was there that he would meet and marry the daughter of one of the areas wealthiest plantation owners, a Mr. Meverell Hulse.

Meverell Hulse was born in England in 1630, having listed his age as '40' in a deposition made on January 10, 1670. His father and mother were Luke Skywaler Hulse and Sarah Hulse respectively. Both were born in England around 1600 and died in England about 1670. Meverell migrated to America, subsequently arriving in Maryland by the year 1661 when he signed his name as witness to a deed. Meverell was originally an 'Indentured Servant' and a planter of tobacco to a tobacco merchant by the name of Thomas Lomax as early as 1658 and as late as 1679 before starting his own personal wealth. Indentured servants were men and women who signed a contract (also known as an indenture or a covenant) by which they agreed to work for a certain number of years in exchange for transportation to America and, once they arrived, they received food, clothing, and shelter. Following their served time, they were provided with land and other property in which to create their own livelihood and residence. It's important to note that before the American Civil War, slaves and indentured servants were considered personal property, and they or their descendants could be sold or inherited. Like other property, human chattel was governed largely by laws of individual colonies.

On April 18, 1675, Thomas Greenfield of Charles County made a will leaving personality to John Baker and naming Meverell Hulse as his executor and residuary legatee. Meverell was originally married to Sarah Greenfield, daughter of Thomas Greenfield. Best records show the marriage took place in 1665. Two children were subsequently born in Charles County: William W. Hulse in 1670, and Mary Hulse in 1675. Sarah passed away sometime before 1679 of an unknown cause, and Meverell subsequently remarried sometime later.

On Sunday, January 24, 1679, at the end of the indentured servitude, Thomas Lomax granted Meverell Hulse 2,000 pounds of tobacco and a parcel of land on the west side of Wicomico River in

Charles County, Maryland, where Meverall was living at the time. The parcel was part of a tract of 600 acres partially belonging to Thomas Lomax.

That same year, Meverell met his second wife to be, Mary Pearle. They wed the following year in 1680. It was the same year that Meverell subsequently purchased 100 acres called "Burroughs Gift (Burr's or Bures Gift) as well as another 100-acre tract of land called "Hulston". Both were part of the land area known as "Resurrection".

The Hulse family had married into the politically connected 'Barber' family who had already produced a colonial governor of Maryland. As a side note, the father of Mary Pearle was James Pearle, born in England in 1592, one hundred years after Columbus first sailed to the New World.

In 1694, seven years after landing in America, Phillip Lock married Mary Hulse. Mary was the daughter of Meverell and Sarah Hulse, as stated earlier. Mary Hulse was born in 1675 in Charles County, Maryland, making her the first direct Lock decedent born in North America. She was 19-years-old at the time of her marriage to Phillip.

Phillip Lock and Mary Hulse were married in 1694 at Resurrection Manor, a historic home located on the northeast area of the Maryland peninsula near the present-day town of Hollywood. The Manor was originally developed by Thomas Cornwallis. Thomas was from the same family as General Charles Cornwallis, best remembered as one of the leading British generals against the U.S. Army in the American War of Independence. His surrender in 1781 to a combined American and French force at the Siege of Yorktown ended significant hostilities in North America.

Resurrection Manor was built amidst a 4,000-acre farm granted to Thomas Cornwallis in 1650, 20 years before the birth of Phillip Lock. The house was an example of early brick architecture dating from about 1660 to 1720. It was built as a one-room house with a steep stair leading to the upper floor. Unfortunately, the manor was torn down in 1970 to make room for a single-family home despite its placement on the National Historic Landmark register. The present-day address of where the Manor once stood is 45270 Daniels Road, Hollywood, Maryland.

Within the next three years, Phillip and Mary Lock had the first half of what would be six known children, all born in St. Mary's County, Maryland:

- William Lock, born 1695. Some records show William passing away in 1786 in Greenville, South Carolina, at the age of 91. Other records show him to have passed by March of 1761 in St. Mary's County.
- James Hulse Lock. James was born in 1696 and was given his mother's maiden name for his own middle name. Incidentally, James Hulse was the 6th-Great Grandfather of the author of this book.
- Phillip Lock (Jr.), born in 1697 and named after his father.

Following the birth of their first two children, on August 23, 1698, Phillip and Mary provided security to purchase the estate of Robert Harrison, a local landowner in St. Mary's County. Unfortunately, 1698 was also the year that Mary's father, Meverell Hulse, died at the age of 68. Upon Meverell's death, Mary Lock inherited a portion of the Hulston Plantation, thereby making her husband, Phillip, proprietor of the Plantation. The Lock's then expanded their property through the sale of estate of Robert Harrison. They officially called their acreage "Good Pennyworth", which may have been officially granted on December 10, 1714. In fact, there were several land deals completed by Phillip; in 1707 (Burroughs Gift/Burr's Gift), 1713 (Hulston) and 1714 (Good Pennyworth), partially though his business and family relations with Meverell Hulse. By any measure of wealth for the early 18th Century in America, Phillip and Mary Lock were rich.

We'll take a break here to discuss the location of "Good Pennyworth", the tract of land Phillip established in 1714, as well as some local landmarks in St. Mary's County attributed to the Lock family. Historical research so far verifies that our founding ancestor, Phillip Lock, resided in St. Mary's County, and attended All Faith Parish (now known as All Faith Episcopal Church and sitting in the exact same location as the building the Lock's attended). We also know that Lock and his extended family were influential landowners throughout the community. It only stands to reason that several thoroughfares and tributaries bearing the name of "Locke" and "Lock" in St. Mary's County were named after Phillip and his extended family. Additional research on these thoroughfares and tributaries has led to the exact location of the 100-acre tract of Good Pennyworth.

Not quite half a mile due west of the All Faith Episcopal Church is "Lockes Hill Road" running northeast and southwest between New Market Turner Road (MD 6) and Three Notch Road (MD 5) for approximately 1.3 miles. Lockes Hill Road also extends south of Three Notch Road for about 700 feet, but is referred to as "Old Lockes Hill Road".

Sprouting off Lockes Hill Road about midpoint between MD 6 and MD 5 is "Lockes Forest Lane" running approximately 700 feet and providing access to eight residences.

Intersecting Lockes Hill Road at the lower third section is "Locks Swamp Creek", a long and somewhat winding stream starting about 1000 feet southeast of the intersection of New Market Turner Road and Three Notch Road, flowing southeast to Lockes Hill Road, then winding northeast toward the Patuxent River that separates St. Mary's County from the Calvert County peninsula. The Creek ends well before the River. The main branch of the Creek is approximately 5.5 miles long. Forking off the Creek are no less than twelve branches, some rather long, and at least two that create good sized ponds. One of them reside just east of the Mechanicsville Post Office.

Historically, Lockes Hill Road was also known as County Route 30042, and Old Lockes Hill Road is also County Route 31193. It began as a 17th Century dirt path leading inland from the Patuxent Path which is now known as Three Notch Road or MD 5. The path led to the various inland farms and churches located in northeastern St. Mary's County. In fact, 17th Century roads in St. Mary's County were no more than narrow dirt paths intended primarily for travel on foot or horseback.

Until the twentieth century, the abundant waterways of St. Mary's County provided the main transportation routes throughout the area. Ships from England transported goods and tobacco to wharves along the Potomac River, and smaller vessels navigated the smaller waterways to move goods farther inland. Early roads linked residents to points along the waterways as well as to government centers, churches, and other residents. Several roads provided access to the state capital at Annapolis after 1695, and to markets in Baltimore and other economic centers outside the county after the 1780s. But transportation via waterways, the preferred alternative, provided a much safer, swifter, and easier journey throughout the 17th, 18th, and 19th Centuries. Aside from facilitating the transport of tobacco and other agricultural products from farms to waterways for shipping (which is exactly what the Lock family did), colonial roads in St. Mary's County also served to connect colonists to the capital, the courts, and to church. Therefore, the path that eventually became known as "Lockes Hill Road" reflects the early road networks in St. Mary's County associated with early settlement patterns that were characterized by scattered farms situated along the navigable waterways of St. Mary's County. In fact, "Lockes Hill Road" facilitated traffic leading from the colonial road to the Patuxent River landing, historically known as Long Point. Furthermore, "Lockes Hill Road" allowed travelers access from the Patuxent Path (Three Notch Road) to the All Faith Church the Lock's attended.

As referenced in the "1802 County Road Book" covering the counties of Maryland, the origin of the name "Lockes Hill Road" directly referred to the late 17th Century landowner by the last name of Lock[e]. The book describes the path as "Beginning at All Faith Church then down the road through Mr. Locks plantation into Cool Springs Road [now known as Three Notch Road] and up and down the said road from the bottom opposite Joseph Parson's lower gate to Dixons (Brotherhood) gate near the Cool Springs." It is this specific passage in the 1802 County Road Book that not only names Phillip Lock as the actual landowner and inspiration of the thoroughfare and tributary designations, but it clearly describes the exact location of Good Pennyworth.

In viewing the general area in Google Maps, All Faith Episcopal Church is located at the southeast intersection of New Market Turner Road running somewhat east and west, and All Faith Church Road running north from the intersection. The actual address of the church is 38885 New Market Turner Road, Mechanicsville, Maryland 20659.

Again, not quite half a mile west of the church is "Lockes Hill Road" which, according to the 1802 book, was the original path the locals took from the church to what is now Three Notch Road. The path itself cut through the Good Pennyworth plantation. Therefore, Lock's 50 acres tract of land was encompassed within the area northeast of Three Notch Road and the encircling New Market Turner Road.

It's also likely that Good Pennyworth stretched southwest of Three Notch Road, where yet another thoroughfare called "Lockes Crossing Road" winds east to west about 1.5 miles from Old Village

Road (parallel with Three Notch Road) to Thompson Corner Road. Most of the general area where Good Pennyworth used to lie is now covered with woods and farmland.

Additional research on "Lockes Crossing Road" has verified that tobacco farming was most certainly a part of the greater St. Mary's County history, as well as that of Good Pennyworth and subsequent plantations. In the present-day vicinity of 3715 Lockes Crossing Road, and as of August 2000, a tobacco barn is situated on the south side about half a mile west of Mechanicsville. Oriented on a north/south axis, the barn is situated in the midst of a barnyard beside another contributing mid-twentieth century barn, as well as two non-contributing equipment shed, and a dwelling. The barn lies on a property that consists of 134 acres. The property is bounded to the east and west by residential parcels, to the south by a wooded tract, and to the north by Lockes Crossing Road. The Tobacco Barn is a circa 1890, timber frame building with a gable roof and rear shed. The exterior walls are entirely sheathed with vertical boards and the gable roof is sheathed with raised-seam metal. The primary or north elevation of the barn is pierced by a double door. Due to the distance of the resource, it remains difficult to ascertain its exact date, although the steep pitch of the barn's roof certainly suggests a date prior to 1900.

Obviously, this tobacco barn outdates Phillip Lock's lifetime as it was probably built 160+ years following his death; even outdating the time of Phillip's siblings and grandchildren. But it represents the category of agricultural products the Locks were most certainly apart of, as well as defining an extended area of the Good Pennyworth property.

Following the death of her father Meverell, Mary and Phillip Lock had three additional children:

- Mary Lock, born in 1701, named after her mother as well as her grandmother. She married William Elliott at a young age and moved with him to his birthplace of Baltimore. They had at least two sons; Phillip Lock Elliott and Meverell Elliott.
- Priscilla Lock, born in 1705.

It was on Friday, December 10, 1714, that Phillip Lock purchased and/or established his initial 50-acre tract of land he called "Good

Pennyworth", whose exact location was specified earlier. Within two years after establishing Good Pennyworth, Phillip and Mary had their last child.

- Meverell Lock, born about 1716 and named after Mary's father. Meverell married Elizabeth Edwards before 1750 and had six children of their own; Jesse, George, Ann, Mary, Elizabeth, and Thomas. Meverell died by May of 1764 in St. Mary's County. As a side note, one of Meverall's grandsons, Edward Meverell Locke, had claimed to have been friends with President Lincoln during the Civil War. Daughter Ann Locke married Baptist Barber, Jr. between 1772 and 1774. Baptist was the son of Baptist Barber, Sr., and Elizabeth Donaldson. The influential Barber family has been mentioned before. Meverell was much like his father, Phillip Lock, and grandfather, Meverall Husle, in the fact that he was an affluent landowner, having accumulated 526 acres in business dealings between 1743 and 1753.

As described earlier, the Lock family in colonial Maryland belonged to the 'All Faith Parish' of St. Mary's County; a Protestant Episcopal congregation establish in the 1600's. Like many old churches during that time, the original structure was built of logs. It was located on the site of the present-day building and was erected around 1655. The building was reconstructed in 1693 and finally replaced by the present colonial brick structure in 1767, 45 years after the death of Phillip Lock. The church building is located in Mechanicsville, Maryland, on the northeast area of the St. Mary's peninsula, and at the corner of what is now All Faith Church Road and New Market Turner Road.

From 1718 through 1719, Phillip was a 'vestryman' at All Faith Parish; that is, a member of the church's vestry or leading body, but not an actual member of the clergy. Phillip was pledged for tobacco for support of the Parish, with tobacco being one of the crops grown on Good Pennyworth as well as other surrounding Maryland plantations. Tobacco at that time was a lucrative crop, and its trade with England and other European countries was supported by the Port of Baltimore as described earlier.

Phillip Lock passed away on Thursday, August 16, 1722, at his Plantation home in St. Mary's County, Maryland. He was 52 years old. His Last Will and Testament created five years earlier read:

"To eldest son William and son James Hulse and their heirs 'Good Pennyworth' equally. To daughters Mary (at marriage) and Priscilla (at 16 or marriage) and sons William and Phillip personally. Wife Mary, executor residence of personal estate. Dwelling plantation Hulston during life. At her decease to two sons [Phillip and Meverall] and their heirs equally."

On the following November 16, Luke, and Edward Barber, of the Barber family previously noted, appraised Phillip's personal estate at £27.3.8. Mary Lock filed the inventory that same day. She also filed an account of the estate on August 8, 1723, a year after Phillip's death. It was then that she cited the inventory as taken by the Barber's, and listed payments of £9.11.2.

After Phillip's death, Mary Lock continued to live at Hulston Plantation with her youngest children, and by then the property had grown. The year of Mary Lock's death is not known at this time, though it would have been before 1765. But shortly after her passing, Good Pennyworth was equally divided as stipulated in Phillip's Last Will. The plantation had eventually grown to 1,200 acres. And by then the Lock family had not only become wealthy in colonial America, but politically influential as well.

The exact location of Phillip and Mary Lock's burial site is unknown. However, recent inquiries to the current All Faith Parish community resulted in some interesting information regarding the Lock family manor home and probable burial sites. According to the All Faith Parish Historical Committee, there are no known burials at the All Faith Parish churchyard prior to the year 1845, and no known Lock(e) family members buried there. Landowners, for the most part, had established family burial grounds located near their dwelling manors. The Committee also confirmed that the actual ruins of the Lock manor home are still in existence! The ruins are located in a field at the intersection of New Market Turner Road and Lockes Hill Road, possibly on the southeast section. To the best of the Committee's knowledge, no search for the Lock family burial ground has been conducted. However, they verified that it is most certainly near the ruins in one of the open fields or woods behind it.

CHAPTER 11:
CONCLUSION

While the Rye House Plot was one of several subversions to undermine the British monarchy during the 17th century, it was certainly one of the most intriguing given its cast of characters and end results. The fact that the planned assignation of Charles II and brother James, Duke of York, was not brought to fruition, never was a failed coup so far reaching in its development, backlash, and consequences: The first-born son of a King twice planning his own father's elimination; a brilliant English philosopher and physician involved in a murderous plot; more than 40 accused and suspected conspirators either executed, tortured, imprisoned, or exiled; the struggles over religious tolerance, and the eventual end of a century of political and civil strife by confirming the primacy of 'Parliament' over the 'Crown'. The end result was "The Glorious Revolution" of 1688; an internal coup and the last successful invasion of England.

While the Revolution was relatively fast and bloodless, pro-Stuart uprisings in Scotland and Ireland resulted in heavy losses. The Revolution put an end to a century of political strife by reaffirming Parliament's authority over the Crown. While the Toleration Act of 1688 granted nonconformist Protestants' freedom of worship, restrictions on Catholics imposed by the English and Scottish Test Acts of 1678 and 1681 remained in place until 1828; while religious restrictions on the monarch's choice of spouse were removed, those affecting the monarch remain.

Thus ended the historic outreach and political influence of Charles II, James II & IV, and James Scott, 1st Duke of Monmouth. Directly related by blood, their intertwined "historiography" floated between mutual acceptance and respect, to extreme disparity and rebellion. Had the Rye House Plot not been planned, James Scott's appointment to King held at least some promise given his position as firstborn son to Charles, illegitimate or not. But his implication in the Plot led not only to exile outside of England, it also inspired the Monmouth Rebellion for which he was beheaded. And had the Rye House Plot been successfully carried out, most certainly James Scott would have successes to the throne per the elimination of both Charles and his brother.

Also related by blood was John and Phillip Lock(e), whose own influence on society and Western culture have remained throughout the ages. Of the two, John Locke was by far the most influential. Locke's claim that men are by nature free and equal revolutionized the claim that God had made all people naturally subject to a monarch. He maintained that humans have rights, including as the right to life, liberty, and property, that are based on principles that are independent of any given society's laws.

As part of his explanation for comprehending legitimate political government, Locke used the claim that mankind is naturally free and equal. This was the outcome of a social compact in which individuals in the wild conditionally commit part of their rights to the government in order for their lives, liberty, and property to be stable and comfortable. Governments that fail to respect people's rights and promote the general good can be resisted and replaced with new governments, because they exist with the permission of the people.

As a result, Locke's argument of the right to revolt is also significant. Locke also supports the rule of law and the separation of powers between the legislature and the executive. Locke argued in his "Letter Concerning Toleration" that coercion should not be employed to convert people to the true religion, and that churches should not have any coercive power over its members. Later political writings by Locke, such as the "Second Letter on Toleration" and "Third Letter on Toleration," expanded on these themes.

Locke's political-legal principles have had a lasting impact on the theory and practice of limited representative government and the safeguarding of fundamental rights and freedoms under the rule of law around the world. Perhaps the part of Locke's writing which most influenced the founding fathers of the United States Constitution was the idea that the power to govern was obtained from the permission of the people.

Locke believed that the purpose of government was to protect the natural rights of its citizens; that all people automatically earned the opportunity for life, liberty, and property simply by being born. When a government did not protect those rights, the citizen had the right and maybe even the obligation of overthrowing the government, hence his credulous support of the Rye House Plot. These ideas were incorporated into the Declaration of Independence, whose original draft was written by Thomas Jefferson, a tremendous admirer of Locke. Once these ideas took root in North America, the philosophy was adopted in other places as justification for revolution.

John Locke passed away 72 years before the Declaration of Independence was written and adopted by the Second Continental Congress. In fact, Jefferson himself was not born until 39 years after Locke's death. Phillip Lock, on the other hand, had experienced the Colonization of America for 35 years; from his arrival to North America in 1687 to his death in 1722. An influential citizen of Maryland, he was a principal figure in regional business, politics, and religion.

Maryland was formed by George Calvert, 1st Baron Baltimore, a Catholic convert who aimed to provide a religious refuge for Catholics persecuted in England, as one of the original Thirteen Colonies. Lord Baltimore was awarded a colonial charter in 1632 by Charles I of England, the father of Charles II, who named the colony after his wife, Queen Mary, also known as Henrietta Maria of France. Lord Baltimore envisioned a colony where individuals of all theological faiths could cohabit under the idea of toleration, unlike the Pilgrims and Puritans who rejected Catholicism in their settlements. As a result, the Maryland General Assembly established an Act Concerning Religion in 1649, which codified this idea by making anyone who "reproached" a fellow Marylander based on religious allegiance punishable. Despite this, religious struggle was widespread in the early years, and Catholics remained a minority, albeit one with a larger population than in any other English colony.

The year after Phillip Lock settled in Maryland, the Colony outlawed Catholicism. The Maryland General Assembly banned Catholics from running schools, limited corporate ownership of property to prevent religious orders from extending or sustaining themselves, and supported the conversion of Catholic children in 1704. Officially, the celebration of Catholic sacraments was likewise prohibited. This situation persisted until the American Revolutionary War ended. Wealthy Catholic planters built chapels on their properties so that they may practice their religion in relative privacy. Individual priests and lay leaders claimed Maryland farms owned by the Jesuits as personal property and bequeathed them to avoid legal limits on religious groups possessing property well into the 18th century.

Maryland's early settlements and population centers clustered around rivers and other waterways that empty into the Chesapeake Bay. Its economy was heavily plantation-based and centered mostly on the cultivation of tobacco, as was the case with Phillip Lock. Britain's need for cheap labor led to a rapid expansion of indentured servants, penal labor, and African slaves.

Unlike Phillip, most of the English colonists arrived in Maryland as indentured servants, and had to serve a several years' term as laborers to pay for their passage. In the early years, the line between indentured servants and African slaves or laborers was fluid, and white and black laborers commonly lived and worked together, and formed unions. Mixed-race children born to white mothers were considered free by the principle of "partus sequitur ventrem", by which children took the social status of their mothers, a principle of slave law that was adopted throughout the colonies. During the colonial era, families of free people of color were formed most often by unions of white women and African men.

Many of the free black families migrated to Delaware, where land was cheaper. As the flow of indentured laborers to the colony decreased with improving economic conditions in England, planters in Maryland imported thousands more slaves and racial caste lines hardened. The economy's growth and prosperity were based on slave labor, devoted first to the production of tobacco as the commodity crop. Tobacco was, of course, Phillip's commodity. While his plantation must certainly must have incorporated slaves, there is no direct evidence to support this.

Fueled by the writings of John Locke, and being one of the original 13 Colonies, Maryland joined the other 'states' in their declaration of independence from the controlling Kingdom of Great Britain, regarded itself as an independent sovereign state, no longer under British rule. This came 54 years after Phillip's passing in 1722. While his political views are not known, most his underlining political views must have harmonized with his relative, John.

The first direct Lock born after the United States became a nation was Stephen Lock, born in 1810 in South Carolina. *(As a side note, Stephen Lock was the author's 3rd-Great Grandfather.)* It needs to be remembered that John Locke served as Secretary to the Lords Proprietors of the Carolinas, and Secretary to the Board of Trade and Plantations. Lord Ashley, a colleague and mentor, was one of the proponents of the concept that commerce would benefit England and that colonies could play an important role in encouraging trade. Ashley convinced King Charles II to establish a Board of Commerce and Plantations to collect data on trade and colonies, and Locke was appointed as its secretary. Locke's role as secretary of the Board of Trade was to collect information on trade and colonies from all around the world for the English government. Ashley's commercial ventures included an attempt to establish colonies in the Carolinas. Locke was instrumental in the development of the Carolinas' fundamental constitution as secretary to the Lords Proprietors.

AUTHOR'S FINAL NOTE

While it is a historic blessing to be related to such influential people as John and Phillip Lock(e), it is equally unfortunate that this revelation was not known earlier while my parents and oldest sibling, Barbara Locke, were still alive. My research in my family's antiquity did not begin until September 2016 following the return of my DNA results. This led to the development of my family tree, which brought me to the discover of Phillip Lock. Subsequent connections with other distant family members resulted in the discovery of Phillip's association with James Scott, thereby connecting the dots between Phillip and John Locke. Most certainly, my parents and sister would have relished in the history of our family and its correlation with one of the most influential of the Enlightenment thinkers.

To think that the ruins of Phillip Lock's plantation are still, in whatever form, present in the fields and woods of St. Mary's County, Maryland, not to mention the roads and tributary named after our direct relative, is enlivening. It is certainly on my 'Bucket List' to one day visit the region and take home a small sampling of the earth once known as "Good Pennyworth". I am also dedicated to not only continuing the research of my ancestors and their interactions with historic notables, but committed to share it with those who are interested, family or otherwise.

CHRISTOPHER LOCKE
7th-Great Grandson of Phillip Lock(e)

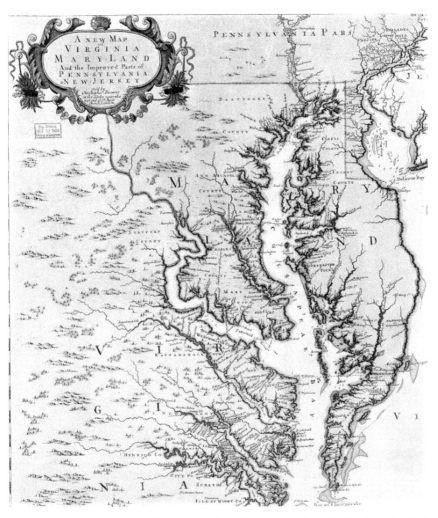

17th Century map of Maryland and surrounding British colonial regions, drawn two years before the arrival of Phillip Locke.

RYE HOUSE PLOT
& PLAYERS TIMELINE

1649
Charles II becomes King of England

1666
John Locke meets Lord Ashley

1679
Popish Plot and the Exclusion Crisis

1683
Rye House Plot;
John Locke, James Scott, & Phillip Locke flee England;
Lord Ashley dies

1685
Charles II dies;
James II becomes King
Monmouth Rebellion;
James Scott is beheaded

1687
Phillip Locke immigrates to America

1688
The Glorious Revolution;
John Locke returns to England

1701
James II & IV dies

1704
John Locke dies

1722
Phillip Locke dies

PHILLIP LOCKE'S
HISTORIC LINEAGE

Phillip Lock, born 1670 (?) in England.
Married Mary Hulse, born 1675 in Maryland.

James Hulse Lock, born 1696 in Maryland.
Married Susanna Stevens, born 1697 in Maryland.

James Lock, born in 1717 in Maryland.
Married Susannah Green, born in 1714 in North Carolina.

Josias Lock, born 1765 in North Carolina.
Married Susannah Hall, born in 1780 in North Carolina.

Stephen Lock, born in 1810 in South Carolina.
Married Rhoda Reeves (Rieves), born 1813 in Tennessee.

William C. Lock, born 1828 in South Carolina.
Married Sarah Ann Hednie, born 1841 in South Carolina.

Samuel Wesley Lock, born 1867 in Alabama.
Married Mary Francis Frederick, born 1874 in Arkansas.

Hildred Albert Lock, born 1905 in Texas.
Married Annie Eunice Jacobs, born 1908 in Texas.

*The L-O-C-K spelling is changed (back)
to L-O-C-K-E sometime between 1922 and 1930.*

Albert Leigh Locke, born 1925 in Oklahoma.
Married Bernadette Henrietta Miller, born 1920 in Detroit.
(The author's parents)

About the Author

Christopher Locke was born and raised in Metro Detroit. He subsequently worked at various engineering companies supporting the automotive industry as a designer and plant engineer, and later in corporate purchasing where he was commercially responsible for the Hemi Engine programs at Chrysler. He holds three Masters Degrees; one from Central Michigan University and two from Michigan State. He has also taught various business and technical classes at the university level.

Chris is the author of numerous books available on Amazon.com. He and his wife, Maggie, reside in SW Florida.

Other Books by the Author, available on Amazon.com

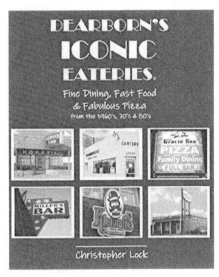

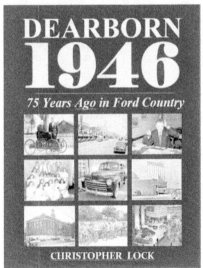

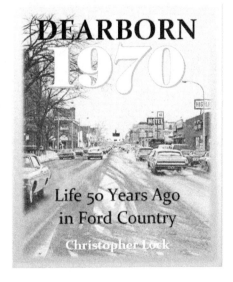

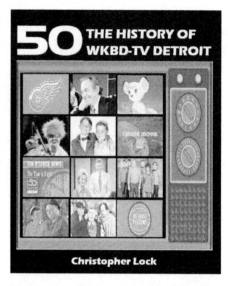

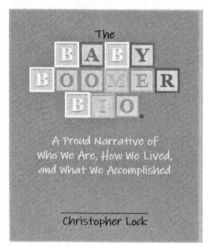

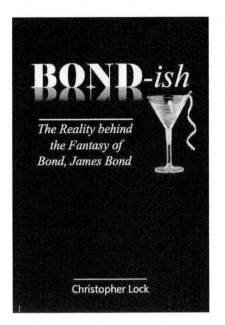

BOND-*ish*

The Reality behind
the Fantasy of
Bond, James Bond

Christopher Lock

From *Kitty Hawk*
to *Tranquility Base*

Sixty-six years of
Human Ingenuity

Christopher Lock

MEMORIES OF A
COUNTRY BOY
1889 – 1902

Written by John Aloysius Miller
Edited by Christopher Locke

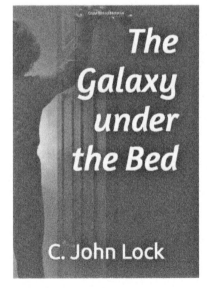

The
Galaxy
under
the Bed

C. John Lock

Printed in Great Britain
by Amazon

11965452R00078